P9-DNS-067

3 2405 00186 4514

SEP 1998

DIVINE GUIDANCE

Divine Guidance

How to Have a Dialogue
with God and Your Guardian Angels

Doreen Virtue, Ph.D.

Author of *The Lightworker's Way* and *Angel Therapy*

RENAISSANCE BOOKS

Los Angeles

MORRILL MEMORIAL LIBRARY
NORWOOD. MA 02062

AGE-8828

133.9
Virtue

Note to the Reader

Please do not follow or utilize any meditation technique while driving a vehicle or using equipment of any nature. These techniques should only be used in a safe, comfortable environment.

Copyright © 1998 by Doreen Virtue, Ph.D.

All rights reserved. Reproduction without permission in writing from the publisher is prohibited, except for brief passages in connection with a review. For permission, write: Renaissance Books, 5858 Wilshire Boulevard, Suite 200, Los Angeles, California 90036.

Library of Congress Cataloging-in-Publication Data

Virtue, Doreen
    Divine guidance : how to have conversations with God and your guardian
angels / Doreen Virtue.
    p. cm.
    Includes bibliographical references and index.
    ISBN 1-58063-025-1 (trade paper : alk. paper)
    1. Spiritual life—Miscellanea. 2. Angels—Miscellanea.
I. Title.
BF1999.V587   1998
133.9—dc21   98-8088
                                                                    CIP

10 9 8 7 6 5 4 3 2 1

Design by Lisa-Theresa Lenthall

Distributed by St. Martin's Press
Manufactured in the United States of America
First Edition

To God and the angels,
with my eternal gratitude and love
for everything

Contents

Gratitudes

This book is a miracle. It is the product of support and messages from God and the angels, and many people who worked very hard to ensure its publication. First, I want to thank God, Jesus, the ascended masters, and the angels for their incredible help in writing this book. Because of them, this book flowed harmoniously and effortlessly, and was completed on time despite my constant workshop traveling schedule. I owe it all to you!

I also must thank Bob Morris, who was the sales manager for the publisher of my first book. Bob introduced me to Richard F. X. O'Connor, who is the editor of *Divine Guidance*. Thank you, Bob—you were there in the beginning, and you've stayed with me throughout my writing career. You are an angel!

As a writer, I am accustomed to describing esoteric emotions. Yet words fail me when I try to express the depth of my gratitude toward those who have helped me. Instead, I will list the names of those who I deeply appreciate for their assistance and support with this book: Richard F. X. O'Connor, William Clark, Pearl Reynolds, Nick Bunick, Neale Donald Walsh, Jimmy Twyman, Rita Curtis, Bill Hartley, Michael Dougherty, Jean Marie Stine, Garrick Lahoda, Michael Tienhaara, Grant Schenk, Charles Schenk, Bill Hannan, Joan Hannan, Ada Montgomery, Ted Hannan, Emmet Fox, Laurie Joy Pinkham.

Thank you also to Debra Evans, Ken Kaufman, Gregory Roberts, Louise L. Hay, Betty Eadie, Dannion Brinkley, Neale Dr. Wayne Dyer, Gregg Braden, Rosemary Altea, Marianne Williamson, James and Salle Redfield, Dolores Cannon, Reid Tracy, Jill Kramer, Kristina Reece, Karen Schieb, Robin Rose, Lucretia Scott, Gregg Braden, Lee Carroll, Jan Tober, Robert Odom, Scott Steele, Camilla Scott, Nikki Kilgore, Dr. Jordan Weiss, Terry Ash, Silvia Aslan, Melinda Stephens-Bucke, Mary Ellen AngelScribe, Forrest Holly, Dr. Norman Vincent

Peale, Phillip Krapf, Dr. Richard Neves, Dr. Caroline Miller, Bob Strouse, Sue Strouse, Dr. Leticia Oliver, Dr. Susan Stevenson, David Allikas, Steve Allen, Gary and Insiah Beckman, Tim Miejan, Cindy Saul, Gerri Magee, Joe and Shantih Moriarty, Andrea DeMichaelis, Tania Chamerlain, Kay Wiltsie, Dr. Elisabeth Ross, Patsy Nelson, June Rouse, Dan Liss, Dale Mann, Elihu Edelson, K. Kares, Dr. Beverlee McLaughlin, Nancy Freier, Steve Freier, Jim Clark, Bo Wise, Horacio Valsecia, Alan Richards, and the men and women who graciously allowed me to write their stories in this book. Thank you all!

Author's Note

All the case studies and stories contained in this book are true. However, I have changed the names and identifying details to protect the anonymity of my clients. The only exceptions are in my own story, and when I have used the full first and last name of a person, with their permission, in a case study or story. In these cases, I did not change any names or details.

When discussing God, I have used the traditional pronoun "He" to avoid the awkward "He or She" phrase. This in no way implies that I am referring to God in solely the male gender, as I believe God's love is androgynous. Please mentally substitute the pronoun "She" as you read this book if this feels more comfortable to you. In addition, some people may prefer synonyms to the name "God" such as *Spirit, Universe, Creator,* and *Father-Mother*. From my dialogues with God, I know names aren't important. The only thing that matters to God is that we frequently have conversations with our Him.

Foreword

By Nick Bunick

Subject of *The Messengers*

At various times in history there have been individuals recognized as very special people to whom God gave a special gift—the ability to have a personal relationship with God's messengers, the angels, through visual or verbal communication, or both. The great historical figures of Saint Francis of Assisi, Joan of Arc, and the eighteenth century's Emanuel Swedenborg were also singled out to receive God's special blessings of angelic experiences.

The question may be asked, Where are the angels now? Why aren't there some people chosen by God to show that the stories of the past are not fiction, and that angels do exist? Why do we not have some contemporary individuals who have the God-given ability to see and speak to the angels, so that we of the twentieth century can also have the comfort and spiritual understanding that God's messengers are not the result of fanciful imaginations of the past, but a spiritual reality in our lives today?

I first met Doreen Virtue at a book convention in Denver. Although we spent but a short time together, I knew from the divine energy and presence surrounding Doreen that she truly did have gifts from God.

Several months later I had the opportunity to spend a day with Doreen in her hometown in Southern California. While we dined at a lovely restaurant with an extraordinary view of the Pacific Ocean, Doreen shared some of her gifts with me. As we sat in that beautiful setting, in what truly felt like sacred space, she asked my permission to tell me what she was receiving from the angels. From the content of the information that followed, I immediately realized there was no way she could have that knowledge other than by divine communication.

As the subject of the book *The Messengers*, I had been giving symposia around the country, while withholding certain information that I had been told by Spirit. All the while I had been searching my soul to determine if the time was right to impart what I had been told.

Doreen said to me, "Your angels want you to know, Nick, that you should no longer withhold the information that they have shared with you. They want you to tell everything, for the time is now right."

I took her statement as evidence that she was a person gifted by God.

Now, I am having the wonderful experience of traveling the country, and participating in spiritual expositions and symposia with Doreen before large audiences. It is an opportunity to witness the wisdom and extraordinary gifts God has given Doreen, which she in turn is sharing with thousands of others. The messages of wisdom and her special gifts have been captured in this book, *Divine Guidance*.

Divine Guidance is remarkable for many reasons. Just imagine, for a moment, that you have entered a beautiful restaurant, and as you look at the menu you realize you are being offered so many wonderful selections—that you are limited only by your appetite and what you are capable of enjoying.

In many ways, *Divine Guidance* is similar to that incredible menu. For Doreen Virtue is capable of bringing wonderment to all of us. Of course, it is your choice just what you will incorporate into your life. If, however, it is your wish to receive information directly from Spirit, that which comes from God and angels, Doreen shows you how in words so simple and so loving that they truly touch your heart.

She reminds you that your mind is the gatekeeper to your heart and soul, and gives you practical instruction in how to open that gate and free your heart and soul to secure messages from God and your angels.

With a compassionate touch, Doreen Virtue explores how each of us has a higher self as well as an ego, and how they often struggle with each other for dominance over our thoughts and decision-making. Doreen teaches you how to distinguish which of the two is motivating you to make decisions in your life. In this book, you will not only learn to recognize when the ego is in competition with your higher self, but also how to modify and control your actions based on Divine guidance.

The insights that the author offers in this unique book should be accepted verbatim, for Doreen Virtue is truly a bridge into the spiritual world. In *Divine Guidance* she offers you the key to open the gate and cross the bridge to the other side. Come join her on this wonderful journey.

Preface

A beam of sunshine warmed the glass-covered passage as I walked to the Minneapolis convention center. The light mirrored my excitement, as I thought of the workshop I was scheduled to give at the Whole Life Expo that afternoon. I followed the signs to the Expo's location in the convention center. Rounding a corner, I saw thousands of people gathered around colorful booths and speakers. The smell of vanilla incense intertwined with melodies from flutes and drums. I never tired of the gathering of exhibitors, speakers, and attendees. The Expo always reminded me of a giant homecoming party.

Neale Donald Walsch's workshop was two hours before mine. Since I had enjoyed his *Conversations with God* books so much, I decided to hear his speech. I sat in the back of the long, dark room. Neale took the microphone and discussed how the voice of God directed him to write the healing messages in his books. The woman to my right began to sob. The woman's companion handed her a tissue and put his arm around her shoulders.

Neale showed great passion for his subject, and he stopped talking several times to wipe tears from his eyes. Several people stormed out of the room during Neale's talk, obviously feeling strongly about his subject matter as well. Yet mostly I watched people's heads nod fervently as Neale gave poetic renditions of his conversations with the Divine.

As I listened to Neale talk about his Divine messages, I also nodded in agreement. After all, his discussion reflected the same messages I had received from God and the angels since I was a small child. I pondered how God seems to tell everyone similar messages of love, like a superhigh-wattage radio station delivering a program simultaneously over the airwaves. God personalizes the messages for each of us, yet their essence is always the same: only love is real, and fear is the only block to our awareness of love's omnipotence.

I mentally reviewed how my work as a spiritual counselor had shifted in the past years. At the urging of God and my guardian angels, most of my time involved teaching clients and workshop audiences how *they* could hear this message for themselves. Teaching as many people as possible how to find their communication links to heaven was important, according to my Divine guidance. These communication links enable everyone to receive important and sometimes lifesaving guidance about careers, health, and relationships.

I thought about the many clients with whom I'd worked who had conflicts about seeking Divine guidance. On the one hand, they strongly desired to commune with God. Simultaneously, though, some people feel that it is evil or crazy to hear a spiritual voice. These conflicting feelings neutralize one another, resulting in blocked Divine communication channels. I reassure my Christian-oriented clients with the Apostle Paul's words in 1 Corinthians, where he calls the ability to receive Divine guidance "the gift of prophecy." Apostle Paul clearly elaborates that, if we use this gift with love, it is a skill to which we should all aspire.[1]

When Neale's workshop was over, I leapt to my feet with the others in a standing ovation. I knew that it was my turn to speak and give the audience another important piece of the puzzle. Just as Neale's life purpose is delivering God's healing messages to the earth, my mission involves communication with the Divine.

As I stood before my workshop audience, their questions unified in one loud voice: "Why can't we hear the voice of God, like Neale Donald Walsch?" Their underlying tone conveyed the unspoken question, "Doesn't God love us, like he loves Neale?"

I looked into the audience's wide eyes, begging for answers to these questions. I was grateful for the time I'd invested researching and teaching about that very topic. As in all of my workshops, I discussed specific methods for having conversations with God and the angels.

Later that evening, I spoke privately with Neale at a Whole
Life Expo speakers' party. A warm man with a deeply sincere
demeanor, Neale shared how his life had miraculously changed
since the publication of *Conversations with God.* We agreed that
our lives always shift and heal in miraculous ways when we
develop a close partnership with the Divine. My own life is a
living testament to the remarkable changes that come from
following Divine guidance.

At the party, a young blond man approached me. I recognized him as the Whole Life Expo employee who had introduced me before I gave my speech. He had sat through my
workshop in the front row, and I had noticed his continuous
wide-eyed expression.

"I come from a very conservative family," he explained to
me. "We went to church every Sunday, but we were never
what you would call 'religious.' What you were saying today,
that anyone could talk to God and the angels—do you mean
everyone?" His face expressed his underlying question, Do you
mean that I can talk to God, too?

I replied, "I've found that *everyone*, whatever their spiritual,
religious, or educational background, can receive clear communications from the Divine spiritual realm. We all can learn
how to differentiate true Divine communications from the
voice of the imagination or lower ego-self. We just need to
understand the clear distinctions between the two. God and
the angels give us trustworthy answers to our deepest, most
personal, most pressing questions. All we need is to understand
those answers, and then act on them."

He smoothed his blond hair and frowned a bit. "So you are
telling me that I can have one-on-one conversations with
God, without having a priest, psychic, or someone like Neale
Donald Walsch translate for me?"

His question brought another smile to my face. I explained
how I, too, had wrestled with doubts and frustrations about my
own connection with God. After I helped him to hear what

his angels and God were saying about his relationship and career, the man laughed, "You know, that's what I thought they were saying to me all along!"

One of the other party guests, a pretty young woman named Kristina, overheard our conversation. She asked for similar help in hearing her own Divine guidance. As we stood in a corner of the party, I acted as a "translator" for her angels, who gave me messages through words and pictures. As I relayed their guidance about Kristina feeling stuck in her factory job, her eyes filled with tears. Kristina shared how she desperately wanted to have a more meaningful career, but financial insecurities kept her from leaving her factory position.

"The angels are asking you to trust, Kristina," I said. I gave her more details about their offers to help her career transition. Kristina's lower lip trembled a while, and then she bit it to stop her tears. After a few more minutes in which the angels shared details to help Kristina lower her living expenses, I saw her smile.

"The angels are right!" Kristina laughed. "I guess I've just been resisting listening to them because of money worries." I then taught Kristina how to hear the voice of God and the angels. As I helped her awaken her spiritual senses of vision, hearing, and touch, I felt a little like Anne Sullivan helping Helen Keller.

The same methods I taught Kristina and my workshop audiences are in this book. These methods have successfully enabled thousands of my workshop attendees to receive Divine messages. My workshop audience members come from every conceivable age group, nationality, education and income level, and race. They are from Protestant, Catholic, New Thought, Mormon, Jewish, Buddhist, Muslim, agnostic, and countless other backgrounds. Just like my workshops, this book is for all faiths, because God sends messages and angels to *everyone*.

As a psychotherapist, I've worked with countless people who have had painful experiences associated with religion.

The common thread for most of these clients is their distaste for anything that reminded them of religion. Most of them don't like any mention of the *Bible*, God, Holy Spirit, or Jesus. These words are painful reminders of their excruciating experiences. Many clients have insisted that I use euphemisms for God such as the Universe, Spirit, or Love. In the spirit of healing, I have complied, if my Divine guidance gave me the go-ahead. To this day, I believe the words we use with spirituality aren't that important if they are love-filled words. As it says in the spiritual text, *A Course in Miracles*, words are just symbols of symbols.[2]

One woman who attended a workshop said she cringed whenever she heard me mention Archangel Michael, because this name reminded her of some painful memories in her childhood church. She asked me to stop discussing Michael so she could tolerate the balance of my workshop.

I talked with her briefly, and I came to understand that this woman thought I was using names like God, Jesus, and Archangel Michael as *religious* terms as opposed to real, live beings. When I explained to her, "I am talking about beings who are very real, alive individuals to me. These beings, including the Archangel Michael, are my very best friends. They have helped me more than anyone I know, so it's normal for me to talk about them and express my enthusiasm when I discuss them."

Once this woman understood that I wasn't discussing the names she recalled hearing in her childhood church in order to elicit her guilt or compliance—*and that I was discussing real people and angels in the spiritual realm who are alive and with us right this moment*—she welcomed my continued discussion.

I've also been asked why I call God "He." One woman wondered if I was sexist. I explained to her that I use the male pronoun when describing our Creator because it avoids the awkward "He or She" phrase. It's also a habit from years of reading Western literature. I realize that earlier versions of the Bible and other scriptures refer to God as "Mother" and "Father." I absolutely see God as an androgynous force of love and intelligence, not a man or a woman. Please substitute the term "She" when I am discussing God if that is your preference.

Some of my clients and workshop attendees have long-standing resentments toward God. I talk with many people who believe God betrayed them because He didn't grant their prayer requests to save a dying loved one, to avert a tragedy, or to heal an illness. So they spend their lives not speaking to God. Still, they come to my workshops, because on some level they crave a connection with God's love. I work with people constantly to heal their relationship with God—a vital element in reopening the lines of communication. In this book, I discuss ways to heal the resentments or fears toward God that are barriers to Divine guidance.

Every day I receive touching letters and calls from people who have broken through the veils of heaven using the methods I teach in my workshops and in this book. I also know the methods work because God and the angels gave them to us. By no means am I the only person who has received these methods. I meet many people who talk with heaven using similar or identical methods. I believe that these methods are innate and God-given, and this is why so many people naturally come across them. As you read them in this book, you may feel you are remembering the information, as opposed to learning it. These methods transcend every apparent religious boundary, because they remind us that, whatever our beliefs, we are all children of God.

You have inborn abilities to communicate with God, your guardian angels, and ascended masters such as Jesus, Moses, Krishna, Mohammed, and Buddha. This spiritual communication ability is part of your God-given nature. Yet, as with other natural talents we possess, we often need a little instruction and encouragement to put them into practice. You will find both within this book.

~~∞~~ PART ONE ~~∞~~

*How to Have a Dialogue with God
and Your Guardian Angels*

CHAPTER ONE

You Are in Constant Contact with God

Have you ever experienced anything similar to the following situations?

- You misplace an important object—your car keys, your wallet, or a letter—and suddenly a hunch guides you to find it?

- While driving, something guides you to change lanes suddenly, and you narrowly avoid a traffic jam or an accident?

- You somehow know that a loved one is in trouble, and when you contact this person, it turns out that your help is instrumental?

- When you meet someone new, your first impressions accurately predict the course of your relationship?

- A disembodied voice warns you of danger, and you later discover this warning has saved you from what would have been a major calamity?

- You think about an old friend, and, later that day, you receive a letter or call from that person?

Throughout your life, you've experienced many instances of Divine guidance. You may be unaware of instances where God and the angels guided you. You may have suspicions that heaven intervened in certain extraordinary events in your life. You probably also have a few experiences in which you know, without doubt, that God guided you.

The voice of your Creator has never left you, and, in fact, can never leave you. The spark of Divine light created when God first thought of you remains tucked away within you. This light is one with God, which means that *you* are one with God. Through the Divine light, which is your true essence, you are privy to every thought that comes from God's mind. In truth, then, your mind is eternally connected to the Divine wisdom of God's mind.

God and the angels have always spoken to you continuously. They have been guiding, coaxing, and encouraging you since you were first created. Not one moment in your entire history have you been apart from God and His wise love. Because God is always with you, guiding you, all you have to do is learn how to strengthen that connection and tune into the various forms Divine guidance takes in your life. When we do this, we feel the peace and courage that comes from being in constant contact with the Mentor-of-all-Mentors.

Think of it this way: if you were offered the opportunity to have a guide who knew all the answers to every question, who was totally devoted to your happiness, safety, and welfare, and who expected nothing in return but your willingness to be helped, wouldn't you gratefully say "Yes"? This guide, our beloved Creator, is already with each of us. When we get in the habit of having continuous conversations with God, our every action and thought is guided with powerful harmony.

Why We're Unaware of Divine Guidance

Although God constantly talks to us, we are not always aware of that guidance. There are many reasons for this:

- We may not know how Divine guidance sounds, feels, or looks.

- We are afraid of being controlled by God, so we deliberately block out Divine guidance.

- We believe it is something else, such as a hallucination or wishful thinking.

- We are afraid of failing when Divine guidance asks us to spread our wings and soar.

- We are afraid of success because we don't feel deserving of the goodness that Divine guidance seeks to give us.

- We fear that God will reprimand, punish, or manipulate us if we listen to Him.

- Our minds are clogged with judgment and unforgiveness toward ourselves and other people.

- The intense feelings of love that come when we connect with God are overwhelming, stemming from our fears that love leads to pain.

- We haven't asked for Divine guidance. The law of free will says that God and the angels cannot intervene in our lives unless we ask (with the exception of a life-endangering situation).

- We want or expect a different answer than the one we receive from Divine guidance.

- Our attention is diverted because we are overly busy, stressed, fatigued, or influenced by chemicals such as caffeine, alcohol, nicotine, sugar, or other drugs.

Fortunately, once you identify and lift these fears and reservations, you easily hear Divine guidance. And once you understand how to recognize true Divine guidance, you'll become increasingly aware of its presence within your heart, mind, and body.

Strengthening Your Connection to God

We can all have clear conversations with God and the angels. Sometimes Divine guidance only requires a few new behaviors that help to turn up the volume so you can better hear God's voice. There are a number of ways we can strengthen our channels of Divine communication, such as:

- Learn the truth that dispels fears and blocks like those listed above (this book will guide you through this process).

- Relax and know that Divine guidance is natural, normal, and part of your heritage as a child of God.

- Remind yourself to ask for Divine guidance as frequently as possible. Practice, practice, practice.

- Ask God and the angels to help buoy your faith, since trust is essential to receiving, following, and benefiting from Divine guidance.

Once you overcome the fears and habits that keep you from being aware of Divine guidance, it becomes louder, stronger, and clearer. As it says in the spiritual text, *A Course in Miracles*, "The communication link that God Himself placed within you, joining your mind with His cannot be broken. You may believe you want it broken, and this belief does interfere with the deep peace in which the sweet and constant communication God would share with you is known. Yet His channels of reaching out cannot be wholly closed and separated from Him."[1]

What God Says about Divine Guidance

While writing this book, I actively spoke to God and asked for His direction and participation. At one point, I had the following conversation with God, which He asked me to present in this book. My questions are indicated by "Q", and God's answers by "A."

Q: What would You like to tell us about communicating with You?

A: *Do it more often! I like it when my precious children call home. The love that comes pouring forth from your hearts when you beseech me washes over me just as my love enters into you. It is a gift that is omnidirectional, and we cannot give this gift too often or too soon. Wait not on time to enjoy this gift, for it is yours now.*

Q: Do you have a preferable way for us to speak to You?

A: *Often. As I say, that is my only preference: do it often. Yet so many are terrified of hearing my voice that they wait for 'later' to call on me.*

Q: Later?

A: *Yes, when they are in 'trouble.' Of course, then their hearts are guilt-ridden and they call on my name with reluctance in their trembling voices. It saddens me that my children have so much trouble calling home.*

   Have no fear that I will punish you when you come to my loving arms for comfort and assistance. I tell you that I hold nothing back from your holy lives, and this is the truth. All I ask is for your honesty, so that I can truly honor your requests as you would have them be.

   When you speak from your truth, I waste no 'time' in the earthly sense, in fulfilling your requests. But when you jumble your words with half-truths or even lies to escape the 'wrath of God,' I must ferret out and explain to you the true meaning of what you are asking for. This is why it seems that your requests are sometimes denied or delayed. As in your earthly relations, the honesty of communication is the crux of everything.

God also emphasized the importance of taking our time during our conversations with Him. This makes sense. Just as we try to take our time to be present and centered when talking with our earthly loved ones, so too should we take the time to be present and centered when talking with God. Here is how He put it:

A: *So many are rushed, harried, and hurried as they breathlessly speak to me. It is so much better to string the words out over many days, weeks, and months, rather than packing them into a single session during one moment of the week. Talk to me while you are in the driveway, leaving your house to go to work. Talk to me in the grocery store, in the cab, in the walkway, and in the alley. It doesn't matter where you talk to me, or when. Just talk to me, children. Talk to me more!"*

The Law of Free Will

God's law of free will says that we are free to make mistakes and choices without His interference. He won't impose Divine guidance on us if we are resistant to His help. The only exception is if we are in a life-endangering situation before our time.

SUZANNE

As a woman named Suzanne drove home alone one evening, she missed a curve in the road. Her car smashed head-on into a tele-phone pole, and Suzanne's head shattered the windshield.

As an ambulance sped her to a hospital, Suzanne feared that she was dying. The two paramedics in the back of the ambulance reassured her. One paramedic was particularly kindly. Suzanne remembers looking at his dark glasses and curly hair as he held her hand and continually whispered, "You are going to come through this great. Just hang in there, Suzanne. You can do it." His gentle assurances gave Suzanne the strength and will to fight for her life.

Three weeks later, Suzanne returned to the emergency room to have her stitches removed. She spotted the ambulance driver and one of the paramedics who had taken her to the hospital. But where was the bespectacled paramedic with dark curly hair who had held her hand in the back of the ambulance? Suzanne desperately wanted to thank him for giving her the will to live. The two men scratched their heads and looked puzzled. There was no paramedic with glasses on board that night, the driver explained. "There was only the two of us with you. I was driving, and Carl was in the back with you. As you can see, he doesn't wear glasses and his hair is light brown."

God and the angels do whatever is necessary to help and guide us. If that means appearing as a paramedic, they do. Many people have told me similar stories of people who appear during times of crisis and then mysteriously disappear after they settle the crisis.

Yet, in the absence of a crisis, God and the angels can appear to be mute and apart from us. Many times, this is simply because we haven't asked for their help and their guidance.

Letting Go and Trusting

Many people feel frustrated because they struggle to hear the still, small voice within. Unfortunately, whenever we struggle, we block our spiritual communication links with God. We must relax and let go to hear God better. Once you become comfortable with the methods of hearing your inner voice, your Divine guidance will come to you naturally.

As children, we are aware of our contact with God and the angels. We are born in a state of openness and innocence. Many times, we shut down our spiritual connectedness because of fear. Yet we can always reopen our connection with heaven the moment that we let go of our fear.

When Anahita, the daughter of one of my spiritually minded friends was two years old, she asked her father, "Where is God?" He kneeled and smiled as he explained that God was within her.

A little while later, my friend noticed that Anahita was sitting on the sofa talking to herself. "Anahita, what are you doing?" he asked.

"I'm talking to God, Daddy," she replied. "You said that God was inside me, so I'm talking to Him."

How many adults would have the trust and confidence to sit and have conversations with God? Many people would wonder if the whole conversation was a product of wishful thinking and their imagination. Children easily hear the voices of God and the angels because they accept without question. Can we practice this open-mindedness, and know that Divine communication is as natural for us as it is for a child? When we do, God's persistent power overcomes all the various blocks that keep us from hearing and understanding Divine guidance.

Our Creator always reminds us to make choices based on love and not fear. He teaches us, when we allow it, that life can be one gigantic miracle. God lovingly and gracefully guides us to careers that excite our passions and serve a purpose in the world, while simultaneously providing for all of our material needs. God and the angels grace our love lives, helping us to enjoy soul mate relationships. Our Divine guidance heals every aspect of our lives, including health, love, and career.

No question, challenge, or issue is too big or too trivial in God's eyes. When we are willing to consult Divine guidance about *everything*, we are freed to let go and enjoy living. We leave the driving to God, with the relaxing knowledge that He provides all of our needs, answers, and desires through this process. Whether we're asking God for help for what we consider the really "big" parts of life—home, marriage, finances, and health—or we just want angels to guide us to a parking space, Divine guidance is continuously available. Think of it as a twenty-four-hour helpline that never has a busy signal and never puts you on hold. Divine guidance is the source of infallible advice and honest answers.

The true "you" whom God created receives Divine guidance clearly and completely. But, there is also a false "you" in your life. This false self, also known as the ego or lower self, is riddled with fear. It fears everything and everyone, including God. It gives you guidance based on its fears, and this false guidance always wastes time, money, and energy, and leads to problems and pain. Lower self guidance is one hundred percent reliable, just like God's guidance. The only difference is that false guidance always leads to problems, while true Divine guidance always leads to joy. Throughout this book, I will discuss ways to tell the difference between true and false guidance.

My Firsthand Experiences with Divine Guidance

My mother, a Christian spiritual healer, introduced me to Divine guidance when I was very small. She taught me to turn to God to resolve all sorts of situations. I learned that God spoke to me throughout the day, and all I needed to do was listen. Sometimes, God's voice would be audible. For instance, when I was eight years old and leaving Sunday school, I heard a male voice outside my right ear. This voice told me with loving firmness that my life mission involved teaching others about the connection between mind and body.

Sometimes we are afraid because what God guides us to do seems intimidating. This was especially true when I was in my early twenties. I had married right out of high school, and I had two sons. While I was very happy to have children, I still felt that something important was missing in my life. I wanted to make a contribution to the world and have a meaningful career. Yet I could not imagine what I could offer to others that would make a difference. After all, I had no unique ideas, formal education, or special training.

At some level, I was praying to God for guidance. Although these were not conscious prayers, I remember thinking, "God, please help me!" and singing hymns such as,

"Shepherd, Show Me How to Go." In my own way, I asked for Divine guidance.

After all, Divine guidance is an answer to our prayers, or to the prayers that others have said on our behalf. Whenever we ask heaven to help, we receive assistance. Sometimes the help is direct, as when an angel intervenes in a lifesaving incident. More often, though, God answers our prayers by giving practical advice.

I received His guidance one day while tending the small garden next to our condominium. I'd always noticed that gardening put me into a meditative mindset that allowed me to transcend negative thinking. As I pulled weeds that day, I had a mental vision that reminded me of watching a black-and-white movie in a penny arcade. In this vision, I saw myself enjoying a very different life. I was a published author, helping and healing others, and enjoying my life. I knew that my vision wasn't a simple daydream, because it made me so uncomfortable. After all, I didn't think I had what it took to write books and help others.

I tried to ignore the visions, but they continued to arrive daily. Soon, they were full-color movies, complete with details about my life. One would think these images would be a pleasant escape from an uncomfortable life, yet they actually made me feel worse about myself. I began to feel haunted and chased by the visions. Accidentally, I discovered that if I ate a large meal, I could stop the movie. So I began eating a lot of food.

After a few months, I'd gained many extra pounds and was no happier with myself or my life. Every time my food would digest, I would receive the visions and accompanying feelings that urged me to write books and become a healer. I finally tired of using food to obstruct my mental movies. At that point, I surrendered and asked God to help me.

"I'm very frightened," I admitted to myself and God. "I would love to have the life that You keep showing me, but I have no idea how I could do any of those things. I mean, I don't have very much time or money. I'm not sure I'm smart enough to write books, and I don't know much about the publishing industry. But if this is what You want me to do, I will follow Your lead."

After committing to God and asking for guidance, I received a strong impression that came as a gut feeling and intellectual knowingness. I knew and felt that I was supposed to call my local college's admissions counselor. "I don't know how I'll have the time, money, or intelligence to get through school," I mentally told God. "However, I did promise that I would trust and follow Your lead."

When I completed the first step and called the college admissions counselor, I received another impression that said, "Make an appointment to see the counselor in person." Again, I initially resisted this guidance, but then remembered my promise to God. Despite my reservations, I found myself enrolling in college exactly as God had led me to do. Since my husband worked a late-afternoon shift, he agreed to watch our young children while I attended school, and then I would come home before he went to work.

The Divine guidance led me along one step at a time until, very quickly, all of the visions in my mental movie had come true. God always provided the money, ideas, and information I needed. I earned two degrees from one of the country's most expensive private universities. If I had waited for God to "show me the money" first, I would still be waiting! Yet, by walking on blind faith that God would provide, I received all of my material support. By the time I was thirty years old, I was a psychotherapist and a best-selling author traveling on the lecture-and-talk-show circuit.

In retrospect, I now understand that God guides us in successive baby steps. We must be aware of the tiny bits of guidance, and then complete them, before we receive the next step in our guidance. I had felt stuck and frightened because I could not map out how I could accomplish the things I saw in my visions.

Essentially, I had wanted God to hand me a full blueprint for how He intended me to succeed. I had wanted full assurance that I wouldn't encounter bumps, hurts, and disappointments before I'd agree to move forward. Still, I'm glad now God didn't show me the entire plan ahead of time. If He had shown me, for instance, that I would be traveling to New York City all by myself late at night during my travels, I probably would have said, "No way!"

I also found that the *how* of my life plan was up to God. In ways I could never have planned or controlled, I received enough time, money, and intelligence to accomplish my Divine mission.

God Answers Everything

In this book, you will read about various methods for connecting with Divine guidance and clearing your communication channels, and how other people have benefited from heaven's help. All these methods are powerful and effective, and if you practice them for even a few days, you will experience profound results. Within a month of regular practice, you will feel comfortable and adept at receiving Divine guidance.

You can ask and receive answers to questions of any magnitude. During my Divine Guidance workshops, I'm often asked, "Is it okay to ask God about my finances, love life, parking spaces, and such?" The questioners wonder whether some topics are off-limits or too trivial for God.

The answer is that since God is in everything, everything involves God. God loves when we ask for His input about everything. God isn't like a crisis center that only takes one caller at a time. He exists in a timeless dimension. Consequently, God hears all requests from everyone simultaneously, and receives them all without confusion or interference. Everything of God is perfect, including perfect communication.

God provides for all of our needs, including love, material support, encouragement, and sound advice. We never need to fear that anything would be withheld. We are the only ones who ever withhold anything from ourselves. God is pure love, pure light, and pure intelligence, so every gift we could ever desire is produced from this source.

You can request Divine assistance and guidance in many ways. You can say it aloud, write it on a notepad, type it on a computer, dream about it, feel it, or just think about it. You can word it formally or casually. You can even request God's help in an angry tone. *How* you speak to God doesn't matter. He hears and responds to the love beneath your request, and is deaf to the fear that fuels any anger or disrespect. Of course, as we regain a close relationship to God through our frequent communications, we naturally speak to Him out of loving respect. His love is so awe-inspiring that respect is a natural result.

The Four Forms of Divine Guidance

Perhaps you believe that God's intervention in your life is rare and unexpected. God *ceaselessly* guides each one of us, and only our lack of awareness prevents us from benefiting from this guidance. Divine guidance comes in four different forms:

1. Visions, images, and mental pictures. You may receive visions like a mental movie, as I did. Or your visions may come as snapshot pictures inside or outside your mind. These visions can be literal or symbolic, and they can also come during dreams.

JOANN

A woman named JoAnn told me that she received visual Divine guidance that helped her relax during a very trying period. JoAnn's neighborhood is normally very quiet, which she enjoys since she works at home. One summer, her next-door neighbor's air-conditioning unit began acting up. All day long, JoAnn heard loud squeals and whirrs from the air conditioner.

She fumed inside and wondered what to do. So she asked God what action to take to remedy the situation.

When she asked for guidance, JoAnn saw a clear mental picture of a white service van in her neighbor's driveway. JoAnn could see that the van was there to fix the air conditioner. With this vision, JoAnn got a sense of deep peace. Reassured that everything was going to be fixed very soon, JoAnn wasn't quite so sensitive to the air conditioner's noise. She was only slightly surprised by the sight of a white service van in her neighbor's driveway sometime later. Just as she'd seen clairvoyantly, the air conditioner problem was resolved that day.

2. Sounds, voices, and words. God and the angels may speak to you in an actual voice, and may even call you by name. This voice may be either inside or outside your head, and it can even sound like your own voice.

MAUREEN

As Maureen was driving to work, she heard a voice urgently tell her to change lanes. She obeyed the command without hesitation. Thirty seconds later, she saw a jeep driving on the wrong side of the road headed directly toward the lane she had just been in. Shaken, Maureen pulled to the side of the road and profusely thanked God and the angels for saving her life.

3. Feelings and hunches. Divine guidance also comes as hunches, emotions, and physical sensations including smell.

CAROL

Carol, a divorced mother of two, felt a strong desire to remarry. So she asked her angels to guide her to a man who would make a wonderful husband and stepfather. Right away, Carol began receiving feelings that she could find Mr. Right at a certain church in a neighboring community. At first, Carol dismissed this feeling as her imagination. Yet the feeling persisted, and Carol finally followed its guidance.

The second time she attended the church, Carol's eyes locked with the eyes of a tall church usher. Afterward, they talked in the foyer, followed by after-church coffee. They instantly became inseparable, and were married in the church one year later.

4. *Thoughts, ideas, and inner certainty.* We also receive Divine guidance as "knowingness" in which we receive information directly from God's universal intelligence.

CARL

Carl, a Southern California resident in his midforties, was burned out from his real-estate career. Tired of the long hours and the roller-coaster fluctuations in income, he longed for a career that he considered meaningful and interesting. After two years of fruitless searching, Carl finally asked God to help him.

Not long afterward, Carl drove on a busy street near his home. Suddenly, a huge used-book store caught his attention. Carl *knew* that he would work at that bookstore, and that he would love his work. He immediately drove to the bookstore, went in, asked for a job, and was hired on the spot. When I met Carl at the bookstore two years later, he told me that he was happier than he'd ever been in his life. Although his overall income had dropped, Carl was doing what he loved, and that made him feel rich.

It's a misconception that only special or gifted people can talk to God and angels. Everybody is equally special and gifted, especially when it comes to receiving Divine guidance!

Every minute, hour, and day, angels whisper answers to our prayerful questions. God speaks to us from within our feelings, inner voice, spiritual sight, and sense of knowingness. Part of this Divine guidance comes from the fact that God created a perfectly orderly universe. Everything happens in exactly the correct time, place, and sequence. Even atoms do not bump into one another accidentally. Every thought has a correspond-ing reaction, and nothing happens by chance or coincidence.

When you have a thought or a feeling, then, you are essentially requesting a result. Whether your thoughts are about worries and fears, or about your greatest hopes and desires, they all are prayers. The ordered universe delivers everything to you exactly as you ask. God and the angels hope you will choose your thoughts and desires wisely. Even better, they hope you will allow them and your true self to decide for you. Still, this is a free-will universe, and so we are free to make mistakes and cause ourselves and others pain.

Divine guidance is God's way of leading us away from pain and toward peace. Whatever the question we ask of Him, the answer always involves love. God answers us directly with suggestions, directions, or information. He also sends messengers to our side. These include angels, the Holy Spirit, ascended masters such as Jesus, Moses, Buddha, Krishna, and Mohammed, and beloved saints.

Divine guidance is always focused on serving, healing, and improving. It never speaks about lack, fear, or competition. Even during moments when God guides you away from potential disasters, the guidance always comes enveloped in gentle clouds of reassurance.

Nothing is frightening about Divine guidance. We often believe it is scary, but that is because we don't trust its validity. Divine guidance seems frightening if you are currently ignoring God's advice to heal your job, marriage, health, or some other aspect of your life. Though you desperately want an improved life, you fear that changes may make things worse.

These fears are your false self's way of latching onto you. Your fearful ego knows that if you fully listen to God, you will no longer be afraid. The ego consists completely of fear. So, if you lose your fears, the ego loses its very existence. That's why it will fight vigilantly to keep you from enjoying the peace of mind that comes from listening to Divine guidance. Let's fearlessly look at Divine guidance, then, and see if we can't permanently lose the fears that can keep us from fully enjoying the life we were born to have.

CHAPTER TWO

The Source of Divine Guidance: God, the Angels, and the Spiritual Realm

Many people ask me, "Dr. Virtue, how do you define 'God'?"

"What do angels look like?"

"Is my deceased grandmother my guardian angel?"

"Does everyone, even evil people, have a guardian angel?"

Whenever I talk about God and the guardian angels, I am asked similar questions. While I don't claim to have all the answers, I do know where they are, and I know how to access them.

Everyone seems to have different ideas about the nature of God and heaven. Perhaps that is part of God's great plan, or maybe it is because people come from a variety of spiritual and religious backgrounds. Most likely, both are true.

Who Are the Angels?

The angels are thoughts of love sent from God. Since God is continuously expressing loving thoughts, there are an infinite number of angels. They are very real messengers, sent by God, to help us feel peace and joy.

God is the all-in-all, and our spirits are made in His image and likeness. God is all-loving, all-knowing, and everywhere, and we possess those qualities. We are actually extremely powerful beings, yet we seem to fear being powerful so we hold ourselves back. However, in truth, we are one with God and each other. The belief that we are separated from God and other people is just that: a belief.

In the true world, where we are one with God and everyone and everything, there are no separate angels or people. We live in this world right now, one with others and with God. Yet a part of our minds, the ego, is asleep and experiencing the nightmare of being separated from God. While we live in the world that this belief manifests, God sends His thoughts of love, the angels, to help us. What are angels? They are loving thoughts from God.

All thoughts create thought-forms. When you think about anything, an electrical impulse is released. Its charge gathers into a form that appears clairvoyantly like a soap bubble. The thought-form creates, manifests, and attracts that which is similar to it. That is why the axiom, "Be careful what you ask for, because you'll probably get it," is true. Our thought-forms are our obedient servants that manifest into our experiences. The thought-forms do not judge whether what we've asked for would help or hurt us. They simply say, "Yes, Master," and help us to experience in the material world whatever we're thinking about. Fearful thoughts take awhile to manifest into form. By the time problems manifest, we've usually forgotten the original negative thought that spawned them. Loving thoughts, in contrast, manifest instantly.

Since God is one hundred percent love, all of His thought-forms are loving. These thought-forms come to us because that is God's will. These are the angels, composed purely of God's love, light, and intelligence.

What Do Angels Look Like?

Most angels look like their depictions in Renaissance paintings. They have wings and gowns of brilliant light. Some angels have obvious genders, while others are androgynous. There are tiny cherubic angels and seven-foot-tall angels. Some are multicolored, and others are a dazzling single shade of pure white, blue, or green. They exude sparkles and flashes of light, which we sometimes see as the angels move about.

Yet the angels tell me they take on this traditional appearance of wings and long gowns for our benefit. They say, "*We don't actually need wings to fly, and since we don't have bodies, we do not need clothing. We take on this form to help you recognize us. If you expected us to look an entirely different way, then we would happily comply, since our only desire is to help God to help you.*"

So, the angels can change appearances. They choose to look like the traditional angel image with wings and flowing gowns, because that is what we expect of them. In other words, the angels conform to an appearance that will help us to recognize them. But, in truth, they are shapeless and formless—the essence of love and light.

The angels respect you enormously, and they will never do anything to frighten you. If they know it would scare you to see an angel, they will make sure you do not see one until you are ready. Yet, though you may not see angels, they are there.

Guardian Angels

There is a hierarchy of angels, because God's different thoughts of love each fulfill many functions and purposes. This is as true for angels as it is for people. We each have a unique mission, and no one can fulfill your mission but you! Closest to God are the seraphim and the cherubim, whose job is to remind us of God's glory and awesome love. Consequently, these angels glow the brightest, since they are overflowing with God's light of love. Next in the angelic hierarchy are the dominions, virtues, powers, and principalities. These angels oversee the universe and carry out God's will across the galaxies. Guardian angels are the angels closest to all living beings, followed by their supervisors, the archangels.

Every person I've ever seen has two or more guardian angels next to them. These angels are with you from physical birth until death. Even so-called evil people have angels. The angels, like God, see that we make mistakes. Some people appear to make really awful mistakes. But heaven looks past our errors and views us as we truly are: holy children of God. The angels know by holding this loving viewpoint, everything that seems unloving will disappear. We can learn a lot from them!

Nothing you can do, say, or think can ever change the permanent station that your guardian angels have next to your left and right sides. These angels look past your surface personality and human mistakes, to see you as a perfect child of God. It is difficult to describe the depth and immensity of your guardian angels' love for you. The angels say that one way to grasp the intensity of their love is to think about a person or pet whom you have deeply loved, and then magnify that feeling a thousand-fold.

Every animal and every plant has guardian angels. In fact, nature angels provide very healing guidance. That is one reason why being outdoors helps to clear the mind. The nature angels surround you and remind you about your true priorities. You return from nature with everything making sense, because tiny but powerful teachers have helped you.

Talking with the Angels

People often express concern to me about whether it's okay to talk to angels, instead of directing all conversation to God. This concern stems from fears of offending God, or that if we approach Divine communication "incorrectly," we will violate God's will.

Yet, since God and the angels are one, errors in Divine communication are impossible. The angels are unable to violate God's will. Whether you call them directly or voice your requests through God, the results are the same. I also know that God has a great sense of humor, and if we do make mistakes, He merely corrects them. He doesn't punish us. A little later in this chapter, we'll talk about the concerns surrounding fallen angels.

To call on or talk to an angel, simply hold a mental thought or question. The angels hear our thoughts and feelings, and they respond to them instantly. Or, if you like, you can approach them more formally. For instance, some people write their angel questions on paper, or say them aloud. I also like to talk to angels and invite them to enter my dreams with messages, since we are often more open to Divine guidance while we're sleeping.

I recently asked for Divine guidance about how to tell whether I was talking to God, or talking with an angel. I received this answer:

A: *There is no distinction between us. We are all one unified voice that speaks from the mind and heart of God.*

Q: Since you say, 'we,' I assume this is the angel speaking.

A: *Yes, it is.*

Q: And am I also speaking to God simultaneously?

A: *Of course. As we say, there is no distinction between us.*

Q: But what if I just want to speak to God alone, one-on-one?

A: *Then it is done.*

Q: This is God?

A: *Yes, I am Who you called, precious daughter.*

Because God and the angels are omnipresent—that is, everywhere at every moment—they can hold personalized conversations with everyone simultaneously. Whenever you get a strong impression that tells you to improve your life, this is

Divine guidance. Whenever you feel an inner sense that it's time to take better care of something, someone, or yourself, the source of this guidance is God. Whenever you feel an urge to serve the world, this desire comes from heaven.

The "Fallen Angels"

I'm often asked about fallen angels, and how to avoid them. Any being who is operating from a dark perspective will always talk about fear, competition, lack, and destruction. In contrast, angels filled with God's light always talk about love, helpfulness, service to others, forgiveness, and similar values. So, whether you're talking with an angel, another person, or your own self, look for key characteristics that distinguish loving from fearful guidance. For instance, loving guidance is always positive, inspiring, and manifesting win-win themes. If you receive guidance from *anyone* that is abusive, critical, judgmental, or otherwise fear-based, don't listen to it.

Asking for Additional Angels

There are billions of angels in the universe, since God continuously thinks about love, and therefore creates thought-forms about it. You can ask for as many angels to surround you as you like. There are some advantages to having lots of angels surrounding you, because they create a "love cushion." The angels' love and light attract wonderful and miraculous events, motivate others to treat you with love and kindness, and repel people who have an ego-consciousness. You can also surround your children and other loved ones with angels, and ask angels to encircle your home, office, car, or airplane.

Since there is are unlimited number of angels in the universe, ask for as many as you like. Because angels cannot violate God's will, there's no danger in asking angels to come to your side or the side of a loved one.

When you have lots of angels around you, their loud choir of Divine guidance is a little easier to hear. Before giving speeches and healing sessions, I call for extra angels so I will clearly receive Divine guidance as I work.

You don't need a formal prayer or invocation to call the angels to your side. Simply think, "Angels, please surround me," and they are there. You can address your angelic request directly to God or to the angels. Either way, heaven instantly responds to your message and sends angels to guide, love, and heal you.

Your two guardian angels are always with you. The other angels come and go as we need them.

The Ascended Masters

The methods outlined in this book help you to clearly communicate with the great teachers and healers in the spiritual realm. These teachers, who once walked on the earth, are now ascended to a heavenly dimension where they are able to help everyone who needs them. They are available for love, guidance, and answers whenever you call on them.

These selfless servants of God and humanity, the ascended masters, are devoted to helping us transcend our lower self traits so we can attain the peace they modeled for us while they lived on earth. They serve as timeless teachers and role models who help us to be the best that we can be.

Among the most famous ascended masters are Jesus, Buddha, Moses, Krishna, and Mohammed. Other heavenly teachers who desire to assist us include Mother Mary, Serapis Bey, (an Egyptian spiritual teacher, in Luxor), Confucius, Quan Yin, King David, Yogananda, St. Theresa of Avila, St. Francis of Assisi (now known as Kuthumi to many of his followers), and St. Germaine.

Like God and the angels, the ascended masters will never violate our free will. They await our decision to call on them, and at that instant, they are at our side. The ascended masters have the ability to be with everyone who calls on them simultaneously, as Jesus promised, "I am with you always."[1]

Some of my clients and students who come from fundamentalist Christian backgrounds feel afraid to "break the rules" when it comes to talking with ascended masters. They quote passages from the *Bible* to me in support of their fears that one should talk only to God and Jesus, and no one else in the spirit world. I respect and honor all beliefs, and I feel that we should follow what is in our hearts.

If you feel you only want to talk to God and Jesus, then I think that is what you should do. I think it's wonderful w hen anyone desires closer contact with God, regardless of their route to that sacred goal. I would never, ever push my beliefs on another person. I am always grateful when my fundamentalist Christian clients and students do the same and follow their own beliefs without judging others who follow different traditions.

The Avatars

In addition to the ascended masters, there are also some living masters, known as "avatars," who are available to help us with Divine guidance. These people are so elevated in their spiritual awareness that they are like angels on earth. Many avatars elected to come to this planet for the express purpose of helping us, and they have forsworn their own physical comfort while devoting their time to the cause of humanity.

The most widely known of the living avatars is Sai Baba, who has learned how to teletransport, materialize objects, and conduct other feats that come from transcending material illusions within our consciousness. Sai Baba deeply cares about the earth and her population, and he is available for immediate counsel to all who call on him. The methods described in this book are excellent tools for contacting Sai Baba, especially about matters concerning the health and welfare of our planet.

Deceased Loved Ones and Spirit Guides

It's a myth to believe that only specially gifted people can communicate with deceased loved ones. You, like everyone, have this ability right now. Perhaps you'd like to contact a beloved relative to ask them a question or clear up some old, unresolved issues. You can use the methods of Divine communication to send to and receive messages from your loved ones in the spirit world.

Deceased loved ones often act in the capacity of a guardian angel surrounding us with love and whispering guidance in our ears. A deceased loved one is called a "spirit guide." You have at least one spirit guide who has been with you since birth and will stay with you through your last breath. Usually, this being is a relative, such as a great-grandparent who passed away several years before you were born. Your spirit guide can also be a person with whom you connected during other lifetimes.

Spirit guides know how to help you without interfering with your free will or growth lessons. Therefore, a spirit guide will never make a decision for you. They will, instead, help you to see your different options and then urge you to make decisions based on love and kindness. When you make mistakes, your spirit guide still loves you unconditionally. He or she sees your true essence of goodness, despite contrary personality or behavioral traits. Like a loving coach, your spirit guide gently encourages you to treat yourself and others with respect.

Recently deceased loved ones may come to you or into your dreams to deliver messages. These are not spirit guides or guardian angels, though, because they aren't *permanently* assigned to your side. Spirit guides and guardian angels are with us from birth until our transition to heaven. Newly deceased people have not gone through enough training to be assigned as spirit guides. A spirit guide is an esteemed role that requires much schooling in the afterlife plane. Those who have recently passed on are often prone to give advice or exert influence without knowing that this can interfere with the living person's free will.

A recently deceased loved one will give you stronger, more specific advice than would a spirit guide. This newly deceased person may have no qualms about interfering with your free will or making decisions for you. That's why it often takes a great deal of time—such as a family's generation—before a deceased person is ready to assume the role of spirit guide. It's also another reason why we usually find grandparents as spirit guides instead of parents. The grandparents have benefited from their length of time receiving schooling in the spiritual realm.

Therefore, it's a good idea to pray for God's guidance before accepting a recently deceased love one's advice. That person is well-meaning, and we sometimes mistakenly believe that once someone dies they have access to all wisdom. However, when people die, they don't automatically know *how* to access all of the universe's wisdom. This skill takes training, on both the earth plane and the afterlife plane. The fact is that our lower-self ego follows us into the afterlife plane, and so untrained spirits, even though they are loving and well-intentioned, often give advice from their own egos. We must use prayerful discretion, and only follow advice when it rings true.

I have, though, seen instances where recently deceased loved ones gave guidance that can only be described as Divine.

MARNA

Marna Davis, a Central California news anchor, drove a friend to the passenger drop-off curb at Los Angeles International Airport. Marna took her key out of the ignition and used it to open her car's trunk to get out the suitcases. Marna hugged her friend good-bye, and then turned to pull her key out of her trunk. But it was stuck!

Marna twisted the key until it finally came out. However, the twisting action bent the key so much that it wouldn't enter the ignition. Marna panicked. A car honked at her to move, and an airport police officer looked in Marna's direction. How could she possibly get out of the busy airport?

Marna instantly called on her deceased mother for help. After all, her mother had assisted Marna in other instances. As soon as Marna thought, "Mom, help me with my car key, please!" she received an instant claircognizant reply. The thought came to Marna, "Put the car key into your mouth and twist it back into shape with your teeth." Without hesitating, Marna obeyed this thought and the key immediately straightened. Marna put the key in the ignition, and as she drove away, she said aloud, "Thank you, Mom. You're an angel!"

During a recent telephone counseling session, my client Kimberly's recently deceased grandmother also gave some straightforward guidance.

KIMBERLY

When I answered the telephone for our session, Kimberly's angels began telling me about her abusive relationship, which I relayed to Kimberly. "They say that your boyfriend has real mood swings. He can be very sweet sometimes, and that's why you stay with him. But at other times he treats you cruelly. You keep thinking that he'll stop behaving cruelly, and will always be pleasant. But the angels say that this isn't likely to happen very soon."

Kimberly confirmed the truth of the angels' statements. She expressed shock that they had given me this information so soon in our session. Then she added, "I wish that the angels would tell me to leave him once and for all. I don't think I have the courage to leave. But if someone tells me, 'Kim, you have to leave him now,' I'm sure I could do it."

"The angels say that they cannot tell you what to do, Kimberly," I replied. Just then, I clairvoyantly saw a woman appear over Kimberly's left shoulder. I could tell, from many years of experience with clairsentient feelings that help me to identify the relationships of various deceased people to my clients, that it was my client's deceased maternal grandmother. She put her right fist in the air and said with gusto, "Well, I'll tell Kimberly to break up with him!" I knew instantly that this grandmother was not a spirit guide, because her advice was laced with anger. Spirit guides, angels, and God may give forceful advice, but never from a place of fear or anger.

Kimberly was happy that her grandmother wanted to help. I explained to Kimberly that her true spirit guide and her angels wouldn't intervene in her personal life unless she were in a life-endangering situation. Instead, they would give gentle nudges to make Kimberly look closely at her abusive relationship so she could make her own decisions. God and the angels know that taking responsibility for our lives and making our own decisions lead to great personal growth.

Recently deceased loved ones, on the other hand, often believe they are doing us a favor when they make our decisions for us. Often they interfere because of their own guilt about not doing enough for us when they were alive. True to form, Kimberly's grandmother was showering me with words and visions to express her strong opinions. "She's showing me that she's wringing your boyfriends neck," I told Kimberly.

"That sounds like her!" Kimberly remarked. She said how much she appreciated her grandmother's directness, and that this was what she had needed to motivate her to leave her abusive relationship.

So, when accepting guidance from anyone—whether your spouse, friend, or neighbor, or someone in the spirit realm—it is essential to be guided by your higher self's wisdom as the final judge and jury. If the advice is loving, supportive, and feels right to you, then you may want to follow it. But any guidance that rings untrue or that is couched in negativity is best avoided.

The happy conclusion to all of this discussion is, *you are not alone.* You are surrounded by angels, loving beings in the spirit realm, spirit guides, and, of course, God.

Where is God? Everywhere, including inside you. What is God? Love, pure love. How can you contact God? Just talk to Him from your heart. I assure you that He will instantly reply, no matter where you are, what you are doing, or what you have ever done.

You are God's precious, holy child and He loves you more than can possibly be imagined. As it says in *A Course in Miracles*, "Try to remember when there was a time—perhaps a minute, maybe even less—when nothing came to interrupt your peace; when you were certain you were loved and safe. Then try to picture what it would be like to have that moment be extended to the end of time and to eternity. Then let the sense of quiet that you felt be multiplied a hundred times, and then be multiplied another hundred more."[2]

This feeling is just a faint hint, according to the *Course* and my experiences, of the peace and the love that is our inheritance from God. All Divine guidance stems from this love.

CHAPTER THREE

⟨✦⟩

*Opening to Divine Guidance: Healing Our
Relationship with God*

Many of us view God as a far-off elderly man. Like Santa Claus,
God is seen as someone who metes out our deeds, or rewards and
punishments. You might see God as capricious and inconsistent, or
as giving and taking according to the worthiness of your deeds.

When we look at God in this way, we necessarily wonder
how He could ever hear and communicate with us. We project
our notions of time, space, and distance and conclude, "How can
He possibly hear me amidst the din of so many people crying out
for help?" We wonder how God could care for everyone who
needs His attention.

This traditional western view of God is called "dual-
ism." In other words, those with this philosophy see people
and God as being separated from one another. God is in one
place, and people are in another.

No wonder, then, that those who hold a dualistic viewpoint have difficulty accepting that Divine guidance is natural,
normal, and nonstop! But there's another way to look at God
and His communications.

If God is all-in-all, He is everywhere. And "everywhere" includes the cells in our bodies and our minds and hearts.
If God is omnipresent, He is able to be with everyone simultaneously. He can simultaneously attend to all of His children without compromising any one of us.

There's an old saying, *"If God seems distant, guess who has moved away?"* When we can't seem to hear God's guidance, it is because we have distanced ourselves from Him. However, since we are eternally connected with God, we cannot truly leave Him. We open our channels of Divine guidance by healing our relationship with God.

What are some signs that one's relationship with God needs some healing work? The first signal may be ignoring Divine guidance.

Ignoring Divine Guidance

At my workshops, people often describe how they received and ignored true Divine guidance. One woman was in a theater and heard a voice telling her to drive home immediately. She ignored the voice and later discovered that a fire had destroyed a large portion of her home.

"Since that day, I've never again heard messages from God or the angels," she told me. "I just know that their silence is because I didn't listen when I was supposed to." Many people, like this woman, believe that Divine communication is withheld because of instances where they didn't heed its guidance.

God and the spirit world can never stop talking to us, however. How could they, when we are eternally united as one? The belief that God withholds His guidance or only gives guidance to a few select individuals stems from the dualistic point of view. In this belief system, as mentioned earlier, we see God as reigning over us from millions of miles away.

Those who believe in a God that is separated from us sometimes struggle with the idea that Divine communication is continuous. How could God speak to everyone about all sorts of things simultaneously? they wonder. God is the only mind in the universe, and our minds must necessarily be one with His.

Although I was raised in a devoutly metaphysical household, for many years I only accepted the concept intellectually.

It made sense to me that everything and everyone is connected. I understood that since God is *everywhere*, He is therefore within me and every other living creature and inanimate object in the universe. In other words, we are all one with God.

On an emotional level, though, I still believed that God was very far away from me. I saw Him as a capricious old man who doled out favors to selected lucky individuals, and I suspected that if I listened to Him, He would ask me to live in austerity.

An instance in which I listened to my lower self instead of to Divine guidance ultimately had a wonderful outcome in healing my relationship with God.

While getting dressed for a Saturday afternoon appointment in a neighboring community church, a voice outside my right ear distinctly said, "Doreen, you'd better put the top up on your car or it will get stolen." The angelic voice startled me, but I was already late for my appointment and in too much of a hurry to hoist my car's cloth top.

"Then have Grant put up the top on your car," the angel's voice urged. I don't even have time to ask my son for the favor, I mentally argued with the voice. Intuitively, I understood that although my car is inconspicuous while wearing its black ragtop, with its top down, its white upholstery and body could catch the attention of a car thief.

Still, my desire to be punctual exceeded my concerns about the voice and its warnings. An hour later, after I pulled into the church's parking lot and hurriedly exited my car, an armed man demanded my car keys and purse.

Fortunately, the angel who had warned me was still with me. I followed an inner voice that told me to scream with all my might. My screams attracted the attention of a woman sitting in her car who honked her horn. The people inside the church ran outside to investigate the noise, causing the man and his accomplice to scurry to their car and drive away.

Before this episode, I had experienced minor miracles from following my gut feelings. As mentioned, Divine guidance led me to become a healer and author. Despite these successes, though, I had never completely trusted my intuition. Its accuracy seemed too hit-and-miss to rely upon fully. Sometimes, I'd follow an instinct that seemed sure to lead to success, and then slam into a wall of disappointment and failure. Gradually, I had stopped listening to my intuition.

The episode with my car reminded me of the importance of following my Divine guidance. It also taught me that God and the angels watch over us and will volunteer to help us whenever we run into trouble, especially a life-endangering situation.

After my brush with death, I decided to research intuition and spiritual communication, and discovered that hearing a voice was called "clairaudience" or "clear hearing." I concluded that I had heard the voice of an angel warning me of impending danger. I recognized it as the same voice that had outlined my life mission to me when I was eight years old. Divine guidance can also come as visual images (clairvoyance), hunches and gut feelings (clairsentience), and a sudden inner knowing (claircognizance). We all naturally possess both a primary and a secondary channel of receiving Divine guidance. This will be dealt with in more detail in Part III.

I searched for ways to identify Divine guidance accurately so I could distinguish true guidance from mere wishful thinking. I immersed myself in more studies of the *Bible, A Course in Miracles*, and ancient spiritual texts. I enrolled in psychic development and mediumship courses, and interviewed dozens of spiritual communicators, including Rosemary Altea and Dannion Brinkley.

I also poured over scientific research that showed statistical evidence of telepathy's existence. In the past decade, scientists around the world (including skeptical researchers who initially sought to disprove psychic phenomena) have verified the existence of ESP and telepathy.

In eleven successive well-designed experiments, Cornell University scientists concluded that telepathy is a real skill that everyone naturally possesses[1]. During 1996, university laboratories in Nevada[2] and Japan[3] discovered that subjects' blood pressures and heart rates decreased or accelerated the moment another subject thought either loving or hateful thoughts about them. Scientists believe this may explain why a person calls us soon after we think of them.

Interestingly, Dr. William MacDonald of Ohio State University discovered that people who pray have the highest numbers of verifiable telepathic instances. Dr. MacDonald[4] explains his finding by saying that prayer is, in a sense, "mind-to-mind communication with God."

My experiences and research helped to move me from a state of skepticism mixed with hopefulness into a state where I *knew* that Divine communication was natural and beneficial. I developed the habit of regularly asking for guidance on matters such as parenting, health, my career, and directions while driving my car.

Though I firmly knew that God answered my every request, I did not firmly believe He had my best interests at heart. My lower-self ego still viewed God with suspicion, and I was still prone to listening to its voice. Whenever I'd listen to my ego, I would wonder, "Will God take away my desires for success and security?" I thought that if I earnestly followed my Divine guidance, my motivational energy would drop. I pictured God influencing me to compromise on my lifestyle, relegating me to mediocrity. I believed that God's will and my will were miles apart.

One evening, as I shopped with a friend at a bookstore, I remarked how upset I felt to see other authors' books get more attention than my own books. These feelings clearly stemmed from my ego, which, like all egos, doesn't believe that there's enough to go around. So, the ego is the root of all competitive and jealous feelings.

I pointed to the "New Non-Fiction" section, in which dozens of books similar to my own were displayed with their covers facing the aisle. My books were relegated to spine-out display in sections far in the back of the store. Still listening to the voice of my lower-self ego, I wailed to my friend about the unfairness of the situation.

Quite innocently, she turned to me and said, "Maybe it's God's will." My skin twisted with heat and perspiration at her words. Nausea and tears both rushed to the surface and I said, "Please, let's get out of here, now." My friend asked what was wrong, but I was too distressed to elaborate.

When I got home, I jumped face-first onto my bed pillows and screamed at God for his indifference to my career. I sobbed that I was going to leave God's universe and go somewhere where He couldn't control me. I meant it, too. I was sick of God ignoring my hard work and goals. I cried and cried at how unfair God was to help other authors while negating me. Why did He love other people more? Was I that bad a person? Was this some sort of test? I pictured Him thinking, "Now, this lack of success is for your own good, Doreen."

As I cried, I tried to figure out how to leave God's sphere of influence. Yet no matter what I thought about, I realized that God would always be with me. Even if I were to die or go into a coma, God and His will would overlap mine. At this realization, I drew a quick breath and found that I was now too intrigued to cry.

Then it hit me. Since God and His will were omnipresent, that meant God's will was identical with my own will. "God's will and my will are one!" I gasped. A wave of tightness lifted from my back and head, and I felt a new sense of freedom. I realized that God wasn't trying to keep me down, because God's will could never be separate from my will. What the true "I" wanted, God wanted for me also. My lower-self's will, being from an unreal source, was the only thing different from God's will. But since my lower self wants only painful things, and desires after meaningless goals that do not yield fulfillment, this will was not my true will.

My whole viewpoint shifted dramatically after that night of hitting bottom with my ego. Feelings of competition or jealousy toward others don't even arise in me anymore. In-stead, whenever I hear about someone who is contributing to the light and love of the world, I applaud them! I now understand that we are all vitally needed in God's great plan. My cooperative outlook brings me great peace whereas my former competitive outlook created pain for me.

This striving for and then making peace with God is known as going through a dark night of the soul. Many people on the path of enlightenment have this experience and, consistently, the dark night of the soul leads to intense light in one's life.

In the days that followed, I turned increasingly to God and the angels. I prayed fervently to be healed of any remaining beliefs and blocks that kept me from having full faith in God. I made these requests without full faith that God could truly help me. For some reason, I'd always thought that God came to our assistance only *after* we had faith that He would. I thought full faith was God's prerequisite. I prayed, "Please help me to lose the fears that keep me from having full faith," before going to bed one evening. The next morning I awoke feeling strong in my faith. God helped me to increase my faith, just as I'd requested. He worked seamlessly behind the scenes and I became more faith-filled without quite understanding how it had happened.

Watching, Not Judging

I also resolved some anxiety I'd had from knowing that God, the angels, and the spirit world were watching over me. Maybe because I'd been raised to believe that Santa Claus watched me all year long and then rewarded me at Christmas based on my performance, it bothered me to think that heavenly deities observed me as though I were in a fishbowl. Yes, of course, I liked them to look after me in dangerous situations. But the rest of the time, I preferred they leave me to my own devices.

Each time the angelic voices talked to me, I was jerked back to the realization that I was on heavenly display. It reminded me of the time right after my grandfather's passing, when as a young, modest girl, I worried he could see me taking a shower or undressing. I wanted privacy and control, and Divine guidance seemed more like interference than a comfort.

Again, I prayed for peace about the situation. I listened for answers and guidance with full faith that whatever questions I asked would be answered. My answer came as a knowingness that entered my thoughts more quietly than a whisper. Through this technique of thought transfer, God and the angels taught me that the spirit world views us much differently than we view ourselves. They aren't out to control, judge, or embarrass us.

God, the angels, the ascended masters, and our deceased loved ones don't see us as flesh and bones. They see our true spirits, and they watch how our thought-forms affect our self-images and future decisions. They do not intervene capriciously in our lives. Rather, they answer our prayers for help by giving us heartfelt guidance.

God and the angels also love us unconditionally. Only our lower self judges the mistakes that we and others make. Yet God and the angels don't have this lower-self capacity to judge. Why would they? They see the unreality of the ego. They have no fear, and they especially do not have fear that they could lose anything, which is the core of any judgment. When God and the spirit world watch over us, they do so with beaming approval and a loving desire to help.

Healing the Belief in Neglect

Although the spirit world is constantly with us and always watching us, many people believe that God is neglecting them.

This belief stems from thinking God is a distant deity who favors some of his children, while ignoring others.

Holding this belief is a source of needless pain. While writing my doctoral dissertation about child abuse, I discovered a good deal of research that concludes *neglect* is the most damaging form of abuse a child can endure. Neglect erodes children's self-esteem more than other forms of child abuse, including sexual abuse and physical abuse.

Researchers find that this is especially true among children who are neglected inconsistently. These children are unable to predict when they will receive poor treatment from their parents and when they will be well-treated. These children then feel out-of-control, confused, and unable to predict what will happen to them.

Many of us have felt inconsistently neglected by God. At times, it seems that God answers our prayers. At other times, He seems deaf to our pleas for help. Believing that our heavenly parent is neglecting us has deeply affected us. Our beliefs that God is neglecting us lower our self-esteem and energy levels, and affect our moods.

What we must know, though, is that God has never neglected us. It is we who have neglected God. Through our amnesia or unwillingness to contact God about matters great and small, we have muted His voice. Through our free-will choices about life and death, we have assumed that He was responsible for taking people and opportunities away from us. We have assumed that other people are reaping His harvest of abundance more than we are. And we mistakenly concluded from these incorrect observations that God doesn't care. These beliefs that there isn't enough to go around also trigger crime, war, and compe-tition. My prayer is that we will all learn what abundance comes to us when we work in partnership with God and the angels.

The angels are here among us to teach us that God is very real and that He always loves us. Their message is clear: we must be willing to ask for Divine assistance, because God and the angels cannot give help without our express permission. We must also be open to hearing answers which may differ from our expectations.

Healing from the Effects of Religious Abuse

As a psychotherapist, I have worked with clients who had suffered from religion abuse. The forms of this abuse varied. Some people were forced to attend churches against their will. Others suffered from listening to hellfire-and-damnation sermons. Some absorbed preachings that told them they were miserable sinners. I have also worked with clients who had suffered enormously from their involvement in cults.

Most of us have suffered pain in our relationship with God. God is not the source of this pain; rather, our *interpretation* of God triggers it. When we view God as painful, punitive, or vengeful we naturally shy away from communicating with Him. Our projection that He is out to punish, control, or criticize us creates our feelings of fear about God. It's only when we get to know God that we understand He lovingly guides us and merely corrects, not punishes, our mistakes.

Survivors of religious abuse can heal the scars which keep them from being open to Divine guidance. The first step is to become *willing* to be healed. Sometimes, after all, we hang on to hurt and pain as a form of revenge. It's a way of saying to God and the people associated with a religion that has hurt us, "See what you've done to me? Don't you feel horrible for hurting me so badly?" Beneath this desire for revenge is a reaching out to God and a desire for others to feel sorry for you—in other words, to love you.

When we can transcend this desire to get back at God and members of organized religion, we come to the next step: to become willing to forgive them. Forgiveness doesn't mean that we have to approve of the actions that took place. You don't need to say, "It doesn't matter what they did to me." Forgiveness merely says, "I am no longer willing to carry around pain surrounding this issue." You choose to forgive so you can have peace instead of pain.

It's helpful to visualize the angels surrounding you as you are healing from religious abuse. See the angels carrying beautiful little baskets labeled "God and Religion." Visualize yourself placing all of your feelings on that subject inside the baskets, and watch the angels whisk all heaviness away from you. Feel yourself becoming lighter and lighter as you empty the pockets of your soul into the baskets. See the angels smile with delight as they help you to transcend all lower-self feelings toward God.

From personal and clinical experiences, I discovered that the key to opening Divine communication channels is healing our relationships with our true self and with heaven. Many people have deep fears that if they reconnect with God, they will suffer punishment for their misdeeds or defection from God.

JEFFERY

Jeffrey approached me after attending one of my workshops and told me that he deeply desired to reconnect with God. "But how can I?" he asked imploringly. "God completely abandoned me when I was a child!"

Jeffrey explained that, when he was nine years old, his parents were divorced. He prayed continually that God would reunite his mother and father, but to no avail. After that, Jeffrey stopped speaking to God. Jeffrey also assumed that God had stopped speaking to him, since he heard no inner voices or other signs of Divine communication.

Jeffrey's fury toward God obviously hadn't dissipated over the thirty years since his parent's divorce. As he talked about God, his voice was intense and emotional. Jeffrey's eyes were wide, like a person who felt trapped and frightened. I saw that Jeffrey desperately wanted to reconnect with God, but was unsure whether He could be trusted.

"Tell God you're angry with him," I told Jeffrey.

"Huh?" he blinked in disbelief.

"Yes," I continued. "I want you to level with God. Hash it out with Him. After all, He already knows how you think and feel. The only way for you to heal your relationship with God is for you to be perfectly honest with Him about your feelings. Hold nothing back."

"Then it's okay to tell God that you're angry with Him?" Jeffrey explained that he feared retribution for openly making this admission.

"Believe me, God already knows you're angry with Him." I explained that God always hears the love that is beneath our every word and action. Even if we speak to God in tones of fury, He only hears the love within our emotion. God is thrilled whenever we talk to Him. If we only show God an insincere smile plastered on our face, we have essentially said to God, "I don't trust you with my feelings, and I don't feel comfortable being myself around you."

Also, the law of free will says that God and the angels cannot intervene in any part of our life (with the exception of a life-endangering situation) without our express permission. God is unable to help us with our anger and resentment unless we give them to Him for healing. When we bare our souls, He can take away all the fears that keep us locked in painful anger.

The next time I saw Jeffrey, he looked radiantly peaceful. The tension in his face was gone, and he smiled from the depths of his soul.

"I take it that you had your talk with God," I said.

"Yep. I was pretty afraid to come clean with Him for about an hour or so after I talked with you. You know, I was raised to believe that God was vengeful. But, after a while, I couldn't contain the years of anger toward Him. I said, 'God, I hope you don't take this the wrong way, because I mean this with all the respect in the world. But you really let me down when you allowed my parents to get a divorce, and I've never forgiven you for it!'"

Jeffrey said that he felt his body pulsate when he spoke these words to God. He felt scooped up in a wave of love. After about an hour, he fell into a deep sleep, and awoke later completely at peace. "I know that God spoke to me in my sleep," he explained. "I'm not sure what He said to me. It doesn't even matter. All I know is that I now feel one hundred percent better than I've ever felt in my life!"

It's There Whenever You're Ready

When you are ready to hear Divine guidance, it comes automatically. If you are a little frightened or intimidated about what you may hear, then God's voice will sound like a faint whisper. Again, this is at your request.

The first step in Divine communication is to make sure that you *truly* desire guidance from God and the angels. They answer all prayers, so if you half-pray for guidance while simultaneously half-praying, "But I really don't want you to interfere in my life," heaven will honor both prayers. To receive complete guidance, a request for assistance must be complete.

Fortunately, if you have doubts and wavering faith, God and the angels will help you to heal these blocks to Divine communication. That's why a logical starting point in developing crystal clear Divine communication is to ask for assistance in healing away fears, doubts, and lack of faith. You will be amazed at how rapidly you feel faith-filled, after making this request.

There is no one correct way to ask heaven to help you have more faith. All that is needed is sincerity. It is probably helpful to be alone in a quiet environment, but it's certainly not required. If you ask wholeheartedly for help, it doesn't matter if you are on an airplane, in a noisy bus terminal, or in an office cubicle. God is everywhere you are, and merely awaits your request for assistance.

Supply in your own words, or simply ask,

P R A Y E R
TO BEGIN COMMUNICATION

Dearest God,

Please help me to release the fears that keep me from hearing Your guidance and feeling Your love. Please help me to release the fears that keep me from enjoying full faith in You and in myself.

Thank You and Amen.

It *will* be done.

~∞ PART TWO ∞~

How to Know If It's True Guidance

CHAPTER FOUR

⌒∞⌒

Divine Guidance and Your Higher Self

To receive accurate and reliable guidance consistently, it's important to recognize true Divine wisdom from mere wishful or fearful thinking. Once you understand the differences, you'll follow your true guidance more confidently.

Fortunately, the distinctions between Divine guidance and false guidance are clear-cut. Divine guidance comes from God and His creations, including the *higher selves* of you, the ascended masters, and your deceased loved ones. All false guidance comes from the *lower self* within you and others. Let's go over the differences between the higher self (also known as the true self) and the lower self (also known as the ego).

"By their fruits you shall know them" perfectly describes the method for distinguishing whether your guidance comes from your higher or lower self. By higher self, I'm referring to that part of yourself that remains exactly as God created you. Your higher self is perfect, whole, and complete, in the image and likeness of the Creator. Since your higher self is eternally connected to God, it acts as a telephone receiver when God, the angels, and the ascended masters speak to you. This is the source of true Divine guidance.

God did not create your lower self. We made it through our frightening belief that we are separated from God and other people. You might say that much of the world is a creation of the lower self, since the world reflects beliefs in scarcity, separation, and danger. Yet, since God created everything that is real and eternal, the frightening illusions of the lower self are just that: illusions.

Even the lower self is just an illusion, since it is composed of one hundred percent fear. It reminds me of the great scene from the movie *The Wizard of Oz* in which we discover the frightening and powerful Oz is just an ordinary man. "Pay no attention to that man behind the curtain!" he commands, but by then, everyone has realized his show consists of only smoke and mirrors.

Everything that is not love is part of the lower self's projections. The lower self doesn't want to admit that it is fear-filled. If it took responsibility for its own decisions to see a fearful world, the lower self would have to choose another way of seeing. If you were no longer afraid, the lower self would have no function. The lower self is bent on self-preservation, so it has a strong investment in staying afraid. Consequently, it believes fear is outside itself, and imagines that the fear is persecutory. Psychologists call this "projection" *(see chart).*

JOUVEE

A woman I know named Jouvee lives almost entirely in her higher self's consciousness. She is always smiling, one of the happiest people I have ever met. Jouvee says that we should rename the Earth "Love." Since Jouvee thinks about love virtually nonstop, this is what she experiences in her everyday life. She honestly believes the entire world is loving and lovable. She is a walking example of the bliss and harmony that spring from staying centered in your higher self.

Is Jouvee in deep denial or is she merely enjoying the results of choosing to focus on her true Divine guidance? I honestly believe the latter is the truth. Jouvee holds a regular job, pays her bills, and has a family and many friends. You might say she has a normal life. Yet Jouvee sees and experiences an unusually harmonious world because that is what she chooses to focus on.

Does this mean that if we focus on our higher self's wisdom we will ignore the world's problems? Not at all! True solutions come from the true Source. In fact, right now, millions of people are receiving Divine guidance that will heal the environment, political structures, economies, and cultural clashes.

CHARACTERISTICS OF HIGHER AND LOWER SELF

HIGHER SELF	LOWER SELF
Loving	*Jealous*
Confident	*Insecure*
Fulfilled	*Believes it is lacking*
Urges you to fulfill your Divine purpose	*Wants you to delay life purpose*
Interested in win-win	*Believes in win-lose / Competitive*
Secure in relationships	*Fears abandonment*
Has a clear conscience	*Feels guilty*
Is guided in its actions by love	*Schemes and manipulates*
Focused on the present moment	*Focused on the future*
Consistent	*Impulsive and inconsistent*
Makes you feel warm and protected	*Makes you feel cold and prickly*
Has a positive voice, even when it is warning you of danger	*Has an abusive and demanding voice*
Generous	*Greedy*
Surefooted	*Clumsy*

Staying on Course

Of course, good can come from anything, even from listening to our lower self's guidance. After all, what better way to learn how to recognize false guidance than to have followed it?

We've all had instances where we listened to its voice and suffered the consequences. Often, we've wished we'd obeyed our higher self's guidance. Either way, though, we learn and grow. So let's not punish ourselves when we make occasional errors in judgment.

We all make mistakes, yet those mistakes, since they are based on the ego, have no true impact on the real world of God. Everything made by God is perfect, eternal, and real. The ego can never change those facts. That's why mistakes require correction, not punishment.

When you follow true guidance, your lower self will try to trip you along the way. Let's say you receive Divine guidance to open a new business. You know that it's guidance from God and the angels because it comes so forcefully, repeatedly, and lovingly. So you happily begin the new venture. Although a part of you feels a little intimidated by the bigness of the project, you are also excited and happy.

Your ego, in contrast, is extremely upset that you are taking action based on love and happiness. The ego knows if you succeed, it will no longer control you. You will stop paying attention to its tyrannical dictates, and will instead stay centered in a loving outlook toward yourself and the world. It cannot afford such rebellion!

So the lower-self ego, a very clever entity, devises a way to reenlist your loyalty. It cons you into believing that you shouldn't trust other people. It convinces you to worry about money and your future obsessively. Since you are already slightly worried about your business' viability, you easily slide into the ego's trap. Suddenly, you find that your fears about money keep you from sleeping at night. Your concentration impaired, you begin to make mistakes. Within nine months, you are out of business.

"What happened?" you wonder. You think, "Well, maybe that desire to open a business was just wishful thinking." After that, you have difficulty trusting your intuition.

The guidance to open your own business *was* Divinely inspired. We know this because of its key characteristics: the advice was repetitive, it aroused feelings of joy, it allowed you to serve others and use your natural interests, and it gave you a sense of empowerment. We can liken this to driving on a big, new, interstate highway.

When the lower-self ego's fears arrived, you essentially took the wrong off-ramp from the correct road. This is how we lose our way. It doesn't mean the original road or destination was incorrect; it just means we lost our way because we listened to our fears. Fears don't keep us safe; love does.

The Lower Self's Arguments

In the following examples, you'll see how Divine guidance is direct, to the point, and based on a sense of universal lovingness. Notice how the lower self disputes true guidance with arguments *(see chart on following page)*.

LOWER-SELF RESPONSES TO TRUE DIVINE GUIDANCE

TRUE DIVINE GUIDANCE	LOWER-SELF OR FALSE GUIDANCE
"Turn left on this road now."	*"What a silly thought. That road is out of my way."*
"Go over and talk to that person."	*"That person probably won't like me."*
"Leave a nice tip for the hotel maid."	*"Why should I pay the maid? I'll never see her again."*
"Begin writing a book."	*"What would I write about? Who would publish me?"*
"You are a healer."	*"Only special people are healers. I'm not that gifted."*
"You have so much to give to the world."	*"Maybe I can become rich and famous someday."*
"Volunteer at that children's center."	*"I don't have enough time."*
"Spend some time in nature this morning."	*"I'll go for a walk tomorrow."*
"Call Donald Smith today."	*"Why bother? He probably wouldn't remember me."*
"Everything is going to work out great."	*"What if it doesn't?"*

CHAPTER FIVE

❧

How to Tell True from False Guidance

Whenever you ask a question, you receive an answer. Yet
you've likely had instances where you followed a hunch that
seemed certain. Later, when your actions were met with disappointment, you lost some trust in your hunches. Now,
although you greatly desire God's omnipotent mind to guide
you, you're unsure whether you'll recognize true Divine guidance. "What if I fool myself again, and confuse true guidance
with my imagination?" you wonder.

True guidance will never lead you astray or cause pain to
you or other people. Very often, however, we follow false guidance under the mistaken presumption that it is true guidance.
This leads to confusion and distrust of our intuitive abilities.
Other times we start out following true guidance, but our fears
lead us off the path.

For example, let's say you receive true Divine guidance to
change careers. The guidance is strong and sure, and mirrors
your deepest desires. So you follow the guidance and make
plans to enroll in college courses related to your new career.
Then your fears surface and you wonder, "Do I have what it
takes to be successful in this new career?"

The fears cloud and overshadow your true guidance, and
you begin to make decisions using your fearful false guidance.
When we do that, everything starts to fall apart. Your college

studies would become unnecessarily difficult, which would make you question the validity of your original idea to change careers. Your true Divine guidance wasn't wrong. These painful experiences naturally occur if we listen to and follow the false guidance that springs from fear.

Divine Guidance Is Never Lost

While writing this book, God explained to me how our fears interrupt His communications with us. He likened His communications to compact discs, or CDs, that he transfers into our minds, which he likens to CD players. I was asking him to expand on this thought in the following conversation. As before, "Q" marks my questions, and the "A" God's answers.

Q: So you are saying that your communications with us are like CDs, and our hearts and minds are like CD players?

A: *Precisely! Exactly! I can't tell you how much it thrills me when my words are received as they are intended! So, as I was saying, at times the 'dust' on your hearts and minds causes their 'reading mechanisms' to skip vital lines and data in the reception of my encoded words.*

Q: So we miss the meaning of your answers to our prayers because of reception errors on our part?

A: *Yes, that is exactly the message of this transmission. Why do you think I have sent you recently on a mission of cleaning up the hearts and minds of your workshop audiences?*

Q: That was Your idea? I thought it was mine.

A: *Where do you think all ideas originate from? Mine is the mind-in-the-minds, the heart-of-all-hearts. Yes, daughter, you've heard me correctly. Think not that I am grandiose in*

> *the words I am choosing. I am merely aware of my greatness, as I desire for my children to be aware of their own greatness as well.*

Q: Excuse me for doubting You, Father. It's just that when I heard 'the heart-of-all-hearts,' I thought, 'That doesn't sound like something God would say.'

A: *And such doubts are exactly what I speak about to you. For these doubts lead to errors in transmission, don't they? When a son or a daughter of God speaks silently to him-or herself and says, 'Hmmmm, that doesn't sound like God,' the transmission skips a beat.*

Q: And information is lost?

A: *Information is never lost! But it is momentarily skipped over. What we are speaking of here today is the importance of what you call your open mind. For without this openness and calm, the CD player retains its dust.*

Q: And information is skipped over.

A: *Yes.*

Q: So, when we think You haven't given us the entire answer to our question, it's merely because we've 'skipped over' a part of what You have told us?

A: *Precisely, bingo, exactly! That's what I'm here to tell you. You've received the information exactly as I've transmitted it. What a joy! What a joy! Now, holy daughter, teach your precious brothers and sisters precisely what I have taught you.*

Our fears cause us to receive partial or distorted transmissions from God. Fortunately, we can learn how to distinguish between true Divine guidance and the voice of fear. When we recognize fear for what it is, it loses its power to frighten us. We realize that fear is impotent, with as much power to hurt us as a toothless dog with a loud bark.

True Versus False Guidance

True and false guidance have clear-cut, distinctive characteristics. Once you learn these characteristics, you'll easily recognize them. Look for these qualities (or, in the case of false guidance, lack of qualities) whenever you receive an idea, impression, hunch, vision, or inner voice.

1. True guidance is mature. First, true guidance has a mature quality to it; it sounds like a supportive motivational coach with a "You can do it!" tone. Wishful or fearful thinking is more like a teenager filled with doubts and impulsiveness in a "You'd better hurry and do this or someone will beat you to it!" sort of way. True guidance has a loving and energizing feel to it, while false guidance tears down your confidence and reduces enthusiasm.

2. True guidance is consistent. False guidance also switches from one topic to another very quickly. It will tell you to do one thing Monday, then tell you to do something completely opposite Tuesday. Then Wednesday, it will change its mind again! If you listen to false guidance, your life will always be chaotic. Since false guidance often calls for investments of your time and money, it's also expensive and time-consuming to follow your lower self's advice.

True guidance, in contrast, repeats itself consistently over many days, months, and years if you don't follow it. It will tell you repeatedly to write that book, start your own business, heal your relationships, or take gentle care of your body. I have three clients who are in their seventies. All three believed they would someday outgrow the feelings and voices that urged them to take on certain projects. But they all discovered that the true self's guidance doesn't go away with age. So now, while they have roughly twenty years left to live in physical form, these three courageous clients are finally ready to listen and follow their Divine guidance.

3. True guidance is about helping others. All of us, without exception, have a mission to fulfill in our lifetimes. This Divine life-purpose, or mission, always has a central theme of love and giving service to the world. The mission can take any number of forms, from being a healer, teacher, or author, to inventing something that benefits the world. Many people make careers of their Divine life-purpose, while some people fulfill theirs through volunteer work or amateur pursuits.

So another major signal of true Divine guidance is that it pushes you to discover and fulfill your life mission. When I received visions and feelings telling me to be a healer and write books, I knew it was true guidance because it consistently urged me to make a contribution to the world. No matter how much I ignored and ran away from the guidance, its message remained consistent like the steady tick-tocking of a grandfather clock, "Heal your life, heal others, write books. Heal your life, heal others, write books." I am absolutely certain that if I had chosen to ignore this guidance, it would still be singing the same tune.

The lower self capitalizes on the fact that most people are afraid of failing their life missions. So false guidance will tell you things like, "Who do you think you are to even consider making a contribution to the world? You'd better not even try, because you'll surely fail. Then you'll be ridiculed, bring shame on yourself and your family, and lose all of your money. You'll make things worse than they already are. Don't even try."

JUDY

For example, every one of Judy Truedson's friends, including me, tells her that she is an incredibly talented artist. Deepak Chopra commissioned Judy to create illustrations for one of his projects.

But for a long time, Judy didn't think highly of her sketches and drawings. Sure, she enjoyed doing artwork and dreamed of being a professional children's book illustrator.

But make a full-time living at it? The idea seemed too big, too wonderful, to turn into a reality. Every time Judy visualized herself successfully supporting herself as an artist, she heard an inner voice saying, "Dream on! There's no way! After all, you've got a mortgage to pay!"

Still, her dream continued. Judy felt tormented, as if an angel on one shoulder was saying, "Be an artist," and a devil on the other shoulder was screaming, "Don't even try!" Finally, Judy turned to her guardian angels to help her find peace of mind. The instant that she turned to her angels, Judy got a strong gut feeling to open a spiritual book she had in her library. The book fell open to a quotation that assured Judy, if she listened to her angels and inner guidance, her life would be harmonious.

Judy wrote me a letter explaining what happened next, "I've heard that same idea before, said in a different way—you know, 'follow your bliss' and such. Yet when the angels showed me this quote in the book, this time the idea finally got through to me. I realized that I was seeing everything all backwards.

"My current job is not the source of my income. The job does not pay the bills. I do. My spirit does. I, God, and the spirit within pay the bills and bring the energy of money to me. My source of income is not 'out there.' It's 'in here,' within me. The angels' revelation caused my whole paradigm to shift to an internal focus. Now I can let go of my fears and be the artist I know I am!"

4. True guidance doesn't procrastinate. The lower self's scare tactics are puffs of smoke compared to the mighty guidance of God and the angels. True Divine guidance will nudge you throughout your life to fulfill your life-purpose. The lower self's counterattacks try to talk you into putting off working on your mission. "You're not quite ready to start yet," the lower self will say. It will tell you that, before you can begin your life mission, you must first take another class, read another book, have more money or time, or lose weight, or it will employ some other delaying tactic.

Any time you receive guidance that makes you want to put your higher priorities on the back burner, you can be sure it is false or lower-self guidance. True guidance wants you to work on the important stuff right away. Divine guidance assures you that you have plenty of talent, creativity, and skill right now. It may ask you to get additional training, but it never implies you need education because you are presently lacking.

False guidance, in contrast, says, "You'd better get another certificate or degree, because otherwise people will discover how unqualified you really are." We psychologists call this the "imposter phenomenon," in which the ego cons you into believing that you don't deserve happiness and success. The ego calls you an unqualified imposter who is faking your way to success. It warns you that soon some authority figure will discover your con game and take everything away from you. Please know that everyone who listens to their lower self shares this fear. It does not mean you are really an imposter if you receive this message from your ego.

Since God and the angels live in a timeless and eternal *now*, true guidance is always focused in the present. They assure you that you deserve and can enjoy complete happiness and security right now. God wills to give you everything He can, and with your decision and intention, you can have all the support you need for the successful fruition of your life plan. Heaven backs you up with all the time, money, intelligence, creativity, and contacts you need to make a meaningful contribution to the world. These gifts are available to you in the present moment.

The false self, however, doesn't like the present moment. Again, this stems from its fear that you will remember who you really are. If you recalled your holy heritage and inheritance, the ego would lose its very life. So the ego continually urges you to look to the future for your happiness. False guidance tells you to delay self-improvements until the elusive future day when conditions are ripe for you to begin working on your Divine life plan. The false self wants you to start an exercise program next Monday, become more loving after other people start, and begin your creative projects after your youngest daughter gets married. False guidance always encourages delay and procrastination.

False guidance fosters "delay tactic" behaviors to trick you. When I was afraid to follow my Divine guidance to write books, I delayed by overeating. I found that not only could I use food to muffle the sound, feeling, and sight of God's directives, but I could also keep perpetually busy. Overeating takes hours and hours, after all. You spend time thinking about food, shopping for food, preparing food, eating food, cleaning up food, and wistfully wishing that you were thinner.

The lower self's guidance often urges us toward delay tactics. These include all addictive behaviors. Compulsive drinking, eating, drug-taking, smoking, television viewing, Internet surfing, shopping, and addictive relationships are the ego's favorite ways to drown out God's voice when you aren't ready to receive it. Addictions lead to guilt because, deep down, you realize they are a monumental waste of time. At a deep level, you know that you are ignoring God's great plan for you. We engage in delay tactics because of fears of acknowledging and following our Divine guidance.

JUNE

My client, June, developed an interesting delay tactic on her way to fulfilling her mission. From the time she was a small child, June knew that she wanted to counsel abused children. Yet she was deeply afraid of being unqualified to help others. Although she'd studied healing methods for years, June kept delaying looking for work as a children's counselor. Finally she came to me to work through her fears.

Just as June was ready to apply for a position that sounded perfectly suited for her, she developed a sudden delay tactic. She called me one day to say that she'd decided to buy a duplex and fix it up for resale. She didn't need the extra income, since her husband's business was fantastically successful. June told me that she loved the idea of redecorating a building, and that she was going to wait to apply for work until after the duplex project was completed.

When I gently confronted June about the timing of her decision to go into real estate, she took a deep breath. She hadn't seen the way her ego's fears had detoured her into taking a side trip. When June realized that her fears of failing as a counselor were keeping her from her mission, she decided against buying the duplex.

The key to avoiding delay tactics and other pitfalls of the ego is knowing the distinguishing characteristics between true and false guidance. It's a good idea to study the chart on page 91, or even photocopy it, and commit the distinctions to memory. That way, when you get guidance, you'll be better able to recognize its source. Nevertheless, if you're ever in doubt, ask God to tell you whether your idea is Divinely given. He will give you signs, feelings, a voice, or a knowingness that will clear up your confusion.

5. True guidance is strong and powerful. The voice of Divine guidance is so loud, powerful, and strong that it takes a lot of effort to ignore it. After all, God speaks to us continually.
I have found that the larger someone's purpose in life, the larger their fear about it. Of course, we all have a big purpose. However, some people's lives are designed to affect many people through their books, inventions, classes, businesses, or creative ventures. These are what I call big purposes. So if you are feeling extremely afraid of hearing God's plan for you, it could be because you have a big purpose. And that is the most likely

reason why you could be having difficulty hearing God's voice: you are choosing not to hear it, while you instead delay facing and overcoming your fear of failure.

Sometimes it can feel as if God and the angels hound us when we deviate from the path of our true-life mission. For example, after I graduated from college and became a best-selling author, I was frequently a guest expert on talk shows. I found that if I wrote books and articles about popular topics such as diet and romance, my schedule and bank account consistently stayed filled. From the reader feedback I received, I knew that I was helping others with my written words. Yet I was quite emotionally and intellectually unfulfilled by these activities. I knew that I was supposed to center my work around spirituality, but I was afraid I could not make a living doing so.

One evening, as I watched television, I felt a strong change in the air pressure near my head, neck, and shoulders. My vision narrowed, and the television seemed to be a million miles away. I felt as if an invisible crowd of beings was rushing me into a private room to tell me something urgent. Unable to move or speak, I simply listened.

"Why are you wasting your life like this?" I clearly heard a voice say inside my head. I knew this was not my own voice, as I had been fully engaged in watching television. The voice within continued, "Think a moment about who your parents are, and ask yourself why you would have chosen them in this lifetime."

The statement surprised me, because until that time, I'd always thought of my birth as a random event, a genetic sequencing that had produced me. It had never occurred to me that I had anything to do with the selection process.

"What lessons did you design into this life by choosing these particular parents?" the voice repeated. I thought about the valuable lessons and traits I'd received from Mom and Dad. My mother, a metaphysical spiritual healer, had taught me about the incredible healing and manifesting power of our thoughts and prayers. My father, a self-employed author who wrote books and articles about model airplanes, had shown me the importance of following one's heart in choosing a career. Early in my life, Dad had left a lucrative job to pursue work that truly interested him. The common denominator in both my parents' lives was their refusal to put money ahead of their natural interests.

I was lost in thought about the lessons and strengths I'd received growing up, when the voice startled me by asking, "Will you waste those lessons in this lifetime?" The air pressure around me changed so that my back was so flat against the chair I reclined to escape its grip. I felt a loving power had pinned me down, demanding why I wasn't fulfilling some unknown contract I'd signed.

I panicked inside as though someone were holding me under deep water. Yet the truth of the message also pricked my consciousness. I wasn't running from the angelic presence as much as I was trying to escape what I knew deep down: I'd been avoiding doing what I knew I was supposed to do; instead, I was filling my days with activities without personal meaning or value.

The angelic presence explained to me, through the thought-transfer process of "claircognizance," described in Chapter 17, that we all choose our family settings. Before our incarnations, we opt for family lives that will give us growth and preselected lessons during our lifetimes. Some people choose challenging families to develop patience, strength, and compassion. Other people select abusive families to get a crash course of the lessons of several lifetimes all compressed into one. I had selected my particular family to gain lessons that would help me in my life-purpose as a spiritual teacher and healer.

I reflected on the message. Slowly the air pressure and my vision returned to normal. But I wasn't "normal," at least in the sense of how I'd felt ten minutes earlier. The voice and presence had brought to the forefront all my unconscious thoughts and feelings about my career, my life, myself. If I had stared into a mirror in broad daylight, I could not have seen myself any more clearly.

True Divine guidance sometimes comes in loving but forceful ways, as in my example, that make its source unmistakable. More often, though, Divine guidance is not so confrontational. In fact, even when your angels confront your unproductive or unhealthy behaviors, you sense that it comes from unconditional love. I also believe that these Divine kangaroo courts answer our prayers for help. In other words, we ourselves *requested* the confrontation.

6. True guidance sounds familiar. True guidance often has a familiar ring to it, an "I knew that" quality. False guidance, in contrast, seems out of sync with your normal personality, interests, and lifestyle. Still, true guidance may ask you to stretch yourself a bit and try for a new job, relationship, or home that you may feel is out of your reach. You'll know it's true guidance by its underlying message, "Trust and have faith". False guidance, in contrast, will confront your aspirations and say, "Don't even try."

7. True guidance speaks in second person terms. Most Divine guidance is phrased in the second person. It will sound as though another person is speaking to you. It may call you by name or begin its sentences with the word "You." False guidance usually begins its phrases with "I" because of its egocentric orientation. The lower self believes that *it*—not the true you—is the center of the universe.

8. True guidance feels like a warm hug. If you are feeling-oriented, a warm energy of love accompanies true guidance, whether it surrounds you, or is within you. We call a person who receives Divine guidance through emotional and physical feelings "clairsentient," or clear-feeling. The clairsentient person receiving false guidance has cold, prickly, and even painful feelings.

9. True guidance is supportive. True guidance may, at times, give you news that initially sounds frightening. For instance, the angels may tell you about an impending job change or warn you that a relationship is about to end. However, true guidance will always leave you feeling loved and supported. In contrast, false guidance stirs up unpleasant fantasies about possible future scenarios. These lower-self messages always leave you feeling helpless, persecuted, or victimized. You can distinguish true from false guidance by asking yourself, "Do I feel empowered by this message?" Of course, empowerment doesn't mean winning at another's expense. True guidance involves empowerment in which everybody wins.

10. True guidance is to-the-point. True Divine guidance is very direct and to-the-point. It doesn't waste words, or give you ambiguous messages since God wants you to understand its meaning clearly. False guidance beats around the bush and gives more rationalizations than an anxious salesperson. False guidance peppers you with words, all tinged with fear and anxiety.

11. True guidance comes suddenly and completely. True guidance often comes as a complete chunk of information out of the blue, usually in response to prayer and meditation. One test of whether your guidance is true or false is to retrace your steps in thinking. Is there a chain of thoughts that led you to your guidance? This is usually guidance coming from the lower self. Higher-self guidance may come in response to a question you ask, but it usually doesn't have a trail of thoughts leading to it. For instance, you suddenly think about your ex-boyfriend or ex-girlfriend, whom you haven't seen in years. Is it true Divine guidance that is trying to tell you to call that person?

To find out, trace your thoughts backward from the point where you thought of the person. With false guidance, you'll discover, for instance, that you first thought of a movie star, which reminded you of an old movie in which he starred, which made you recall going to the drive-in theater, which then brought up memories of your ex-lover. In true Divine guidance, you think of the person out of the blue, without the trail leading up to the thought.

12. True guidance never puts us above or below others. False guidance nearly always involves scenarios in which you appear in the starring role as the hero. The lower-self ego tries to convince you that, if you follow its lead, everyone will adore and revere you. False guidance puts you in the starring role, a role that usually has you competing, attacking, or winning at others' expense.

When the true self guides you, you'll play a different type of role. True guidance shows you scenarios in which you make a meaningful contribution with your natural talents. Your material needs are met while you undertake this endeavor, and other people appreciate your work. In contrast with the scenarios generated by false guidance however, your true self will never elevate you above other people. All of its advice is based on the knowledge that God loves everyone equally.

True and false guidance are both one hundred percent reliable. True guidance consistently gives us empowering advice, while false guidance always gives fear-based suggestions that lead to rash decisions. Our goal is to recognize and choose the wisdom that comes from our true self's guidance. The following chart outlines the key characteristics of true and false guidance *(see chart on following page)*:

CHARACTERISTICS OF TRUE AND FALSE GUIDANCE

TRUE GUIDANCE	FALSE GUIDANCE
Has mature tone and content	*Immature tone and suggestions*
Says the same thing repeatedly	*Switches topics impulsively*
Talks about your life's purpose or mission	*Talks about how to compete with others*
Wants you to be joyful right now	*Wants you to delay happiness for the future*
Strong, powerful, difficult to ignore	*Insidious and sneaky*
Has a ring of familiarity to it	*Seems out of sync with your interests and lifestyle*
Usually says "you"	*Uses the word, "I" constantly*
Has a loving and energizing feel to it	*Drains your enthusiasm and energy*
Surrounds you with warm, loving energy	*Makes you feel cold, prickly, alone, or afraid*
Sounds supportive and motivational	*Uses abusive and critical words*
Assures you that you can do it	*Tears down your confidence*
Empowers you	*Weakens you*
Direct and to the point	*Wordy and full of rationalizations*
Comes suddenly in response to prayer	*Comes gradually in response to worry*
Knows you are equal and one with others	*Says that you are better or worse than others*

~~❧ PART THREE ❧~~

*How to Clear
Your Divine Communication Channels*

༄

CHAPTER SIX

The Four Clairs: Discovering Your Divine Communication Style

Have you ever:

- Seen a picture or scene in your mind while awake or dreaming that later came true?

- Heard a sudden voice that warned you of impending danger?

- Had a strong feeling about some situation or person that later proved accurate?

- Suddenly and inexplicably "known" something?

These are examples of the four ways God and the spirit world communicate with us. In the chapters that follow, you will learn how to identify your personal style of communication with the Divine. You'll also receive information that you can immediately use to strengthen the four channels of Divine guidance.

The Four Clairs

Every person has four methods, or channels, for receiving Divine guidance through sight, sound, feeling, and thought:

1. *Clairvoyance,* or "clear seeing," brings Divine guidance as still pictures or miniature movies that your mind's eye sees inside or outside your head.

2. *Clairaudience,* which means "clear hearing," involves hearing guidance coming from the outside or from inside your mind. This is the "still, small voice" within. It may or may not sound like your own voice.

3. *Clairsentience,* which means "clear feeling," involves receiving Divine guidance as an emotion or a physical sensation such as a smell, tightened muscles, or a touch.

4. *Claircognizance,* or "clear knowing," means suddenly knowing something for a fact, without knowing *how* you know.

We usually receive Divine guidance through the same communication channel or channels that we use during our everyday experiences. For example, if you are mostly concerned with what you *see* during your daily activities, you have a visual orientation and are likely to receive Divine guidance clairvoyantly. If you usually pay attention people's voices, music, and noises, your orientation is auditory, and you'd receive clairaudient Divine guidance. Other people experience the world through their emotions and senses, and these feeling-oriented people would receive clairsentient Divine guidance. Those who focus on the underlying messages and meanings of their experiences are more cognitively oriented. Their Divine guidance would come claircognizantly.

All the channels are equally efficient at receiving true and helpful information. No channel is superior to the others, although my workshop attendees usually want to develop clairvoyance more than any other channel. Clairvoyance, like the other channels, can be opened and enhanced through the methods you'll read about in the upcoming chapters.

Everyone has the capacity to receive Divine guidance through all four channels. However, people newly on the spiritual path usually have only one or two channels open at first. After time and practice, they gradually open the other channels. Initially, it's best to focus on the one or two communication channels that are natural to you. After becoming accustomed to those channels, you'll naturally open the other ones.

Finding Your Divine Communication Style: Exercise 1
Here's a self-quiz to help you determine your present channels of Divine communication. Use the first answer that enters your mind, instead of trying to figure out the quiz's answers.

1. *What I first notice about a new acquaintance is:*
    a) How the person looks, such as facial expressions, hair style, or manner of dress.
    b) The sound, tone, and volume of the person's voice.
    c) Whether or not I feel comfortable in the person's company.
    d) Whether or not the person has interesting information to discuss with me.

2. *The last movie I really enjoyed had:*
    a) beautiful scenery or attractive actors and actresses.
    b) great music and expressive voices.
    c) a story that moved me emotionally and left me feeling great.
    d) a wonderful message that made me learn something new.

3. *Which of these phrases are you most likely to say?*
    a) "I see what you mean."
    b) "I hear what you are saying."
    c) "This is how I feel about the situation."
    d) "Let me think about that."

4. *Whenever I am solving a problem, I am most likely to:*
   a) visualize different possible solutions.
   b) talk to myself, until I come up with a solution.
   c) contemplate the situation until I get a feeling of peace.
   d) wait for an answer to appear in my mind.

5. *My ideal career involves:*
   a) artistic endeavors such as painting, drawing, sculpting, photography, architecture, or filmmaking.
   b) composing, playing music, or giving speeches.
   c) counseling, healing, dancing, and/or writing poetry.
   d) research, science, writing nonfiction books and articles, medicine, and/or inventing.

6. *What I most love about nature is:*
   a) beautiful flowers, trees, and other scenery.
   b) the sounds of birds, animals, the surf, and the wind.
   c) the scents and the fresh air.
   d) I don't get out in nature much, but I would like to spend some time alone outdoors.

7. *What I'd most like to improve about myself is:*
   a) my physical appearance.
   b) my voice.
   c) how I feel about myself.
   d) my knowledge about my favorite topic.

8. *If I received some extra money, the first thing I would do is:*
   a) buy something to beautify my life, such as a painting, a piece of jewelry, or new furniture.
   b) get front-row seats at a performance by my favorite musicians.
   c) go on a rejuvenating retreat.
   d) upgrade my computer system.

9. *If I could meet any famous person, living or dead, I'd most want to meet:*
   a) my favorite movie star.
   b) my favorite musician.
   c) an author whose work made me feel really good about myself.
   d) a famous inventor who changed the course of history.

10. *My pet peeve about restaurants is that they are:*
    a) too dark, making it difficult to see the menu and my dining companions.
    b) too noisy, making it difficult to hear the conversation at my table.
    c) too crowded, making it difficult for me to relax and enjoy myself.
    d) too expensive, making it difficult for me to understand why I should eat out rather than eat at home.

11. *I love to relax by:*
    a) watching television or a movie.
    b) listening to music.
    c) soaking in a hot tub.
    d) reading a good book.

12. *When I'm on vacation, I spend a lot of time:*
    a) taking photographs and/or videos.
    b) talking to the local residents.
    c) eating the delicious local cuisine.
    d) learning about the history of the area.

13. *My most important consideration when shopping for a new vehicle is:*
    a) its appearance: its style, color, and design.
    b) the sound of the engine, the quality of its stereo system, or the quietness of its interior.
    c) my comfort and pleasure while driving it.
    d) the rating given to the car by *Consumer Reports, Car & Driver,* or other consumer researchers.

14. *The one essential characteristic of my work environment is that it must:*
    a) have sufficient lighting.
    b) be quiet.
    c) be comfortable.
    d) have a dedicated telephone line for a computer modem or other access to the Internet.

15. *The thing I most remember about going to the circus as a child is:*
    a) the sights of the clowns and the big-top tent.
    b) the sounds of calliope music, children laughing, and the circus announcer.
    c) the smells of popcorn and animals.
    d) wondering how the tightrope walkers and acrobats could stay so balanced.

Now count the number of "a" answers you circled, the number of "b" answers, and so on. If you mostly circled "a" answers, you have a visual orientation; a majority of "b" answers signifies an auditory orientation; "c" is a feeling orientation; and "d" shows a cognitive orientation. None of the orientations is superior or inferior to the others; they are all just our natural ways of relating to the world.

If you had an equal or near-equal number of, for example, "b" and "c" answers, this means that you have two wide-open channels of Divine communication. In this example, your answers would show you are oriented to both sound and feelings. Most people find they have one primary and one secondary orientation, and the other two orientations only received a few answers. For instance, you may have circled seven "a" answers, four "b" answers, two "c" answers, and two "d" answers. This would show a person who is very visual, somewhat auditory, and slightly oriented to feelings and thoughts.

Finding Your Natural Communication Style: Exercise 2
To learn more about your natural communication style, pay close attention to how you react and respond as you read the following scenario:

As you step off a small airplane onto the tropical island's airport tarmac, your senses are bombarded with intense pleasure. An attractive islander dressed in a bright floral print greets you by draping a lei of purple orchids around your neck. As you thank the islander, you notice beautiful Hawaiian ukulele music playing "Hona Hona Lei" in the distance. A moist tropical breeze blows across your skin, wafting the sweet fragrance of Hawaiian orchids into your nostrils. You feel as though you are in paradise. You momentarily wonder about what type of career you could make for yourself on this island, so you could become a permanent resident.

1. *Now take a moment to recall the tropical island scene. What stands out the most in your mind?*
   a) The sight of the attractive islander wearing the bright print and holding the purple lei?
   b) The sound of the Hawaiian ukulele music?
   c) The feeling of the humid air, the scent of fragrant flowers, and the peaceful, paradisical atmosphere?
   d) The thoughts about looking for a job so you never have to leave the island?

As before, "a" relates to a visual orientation, "b" to an auditory orientation, "c" to a feeling orientation, and "d" to a thinking orientation.

Whatever stands out most clearly to you is another indication of your natural way of relating to the world. As you relate to the physical world, so do you relate to the spiritual world. God and the angels use all four channels of communication, yet we usually only notice those channels to which we are naturally receptive.

Finding Your Divine Communication Style: Exercise 3
Let's try another method for pinpointing your Divine communication style:

1. Get into a comfortable position.

2. Take two or three deep breaths.

3. Focus inside your chest. You may notice warmth or a feeling of expansiveness around your heart.

4. Mentally become aware of the angels around you. You have two or more guardian angels with you. They have been with you since birth, and will stay with you until your physical death. You may feel their presence as a difference in the air pressure or temperature next to your left or right shoulder. You may see their presence as a twinkling or flashing light. You may hear a sweet strain of music or a faint, loving voice within your mind. Or you just may *know* that the angels are with you, without knowing how you know.

5. Ask the angels, "Please tell me the name of the guardian angel on my left shoulder."

6. Notice the answer that comes to you. Did you *see* an image of the name? Did you *hear* the answer? Did you get a *feeling* about what the answer was? Or was it a *knowingness*?

7. Repeat step 5 and say, "Please tell me the name of the guardian angel on my right shoulder."

If you received no answer at all, then try the exercise again a little later. The most common reason why answers aren't received during this exercise is that you are trying too hard to force an answer to come. The act of forcing anything to happen puts you into your lower-self ego state, which does not allow Divine communication. So instead of chasing Divine guidance, it's important to relax and allow it come to you.

Finding Your Divine Communication Style: Exercise 4

1. *Let's try another question.* As before, you'll want to get into a comfortable position and take a few deep breaths. Then, after you have turned your focus within, ask your angels: "What changes would you guide me to make in my life?"

2. *Take another deep breath if you like, and then notice what comes in.* Did you get a vision, such as a picture or a movie of yourself making a change? Did you hear a truth-filled and loving voice counsel you to take steps to improve your life? Did you get a gut feeling that told you some area of your life needs healing? Or did you get a knowingness or an idea that gave you instructions about how to make your life more meaningful and fulfilled?

Again, we all have the capacity to receive Divine guidance from all four channels. So you may receive a mixture of, say, a vision with a feeling. *How* you receive guidance from God and your guardian angels isn't important. What matters is that you notice them, can verify their Divine source, and act on it. We will discuss ways to overcome the fears, doubts, and distrust that keep you from following Divine guidance in later chapters.

How to Ask for Divine Guidance

In case you wondered, the reason I emphasize deep breaths is that they are a key factor in connecting with Divine guidance. The word "breath" comes from the root "inspire," meaning to "breathe in spirit." You are literally taking the spirit world into your body as you breathe deeply.

When I met Dannion Brinkley, the man who had near-death experiences after being struck by lightning and is the best-selling author of *Saved by the Light*, he told me even more about the power of breath. Dannion said that our breath is the means by which we receive guidance and instructions from the spirit world. He likened breathing to "phoning home." Perhaps this is why many spiritual disciplines emphasize the importance of deep breathing during prayer and meditation.

The first step to take when consciously asking for Divine guidance is to slow your pace a bit and take a few deep breaths. Many of us hold our breath or breathe shallowly, especially during tense situations. Yet these situations are precisely when deep breaths would help us the most! The more you are in need of help, the deeper your breath should be.

During the next few hours, randomly monitor your breathing. Now and then, notice your depth and rate of breathing. Ask yourself, "Am I holding my breath or am I drinking in the delicious air?"

Commit now to developing the healthful habit of breathing deeply from your diaphragm (at the base of your lungs). Without hyperventilating, take in as much breath as you can through your nose. Then slowly empty your lungs by blowing the air out of your mouth.

When you're ready, the second step is to ask a question you want God to answer. You can ask the question aloud, mentally, or by writing it by hand or with a keyboard. In later chapters, we'll discuss specific ways to formulate questions to God so you receive the most helpful answers. For now, the best starting point is to be sure your questions are truly honest. Otherwise, you might state a question with your mind that you believe is a "correct" question to ask God, yet hold a different, more honest question in your heart. God always answers the questions, requests, and prayers we hold in our hearts. Since God knows everything about us, we might as well be completely candid when requesting Divine guidance.

Third, don't try to force an answer to come. Try to let go, and let God do all of the work. This can seem foreign to those of us who are accustomed to running the show. Many of us have difficulty asking for and accepting help from others— even from God Himself! As we discussed in Chapter 2, if you feel inside that you don't deserve or are unworthy of God's help, then it's likely you'll feel uncomfortable requesting Divine guidance.

God and the angels easily heal these ego-based fears. So a good fourth step is to ask God to heal your fears about Divine guidance. Go within and take a few deep breaths and say the following affirmation:

P R A Y E R
TO HEAL YOUR FEARS

Dearest God,

I am willing to release and be healed from all of my fears that keep me from receiving Your guidance, help, and love. Please help me to heal from any blocks I have that prevent me from knowing Your joy.

Thank You and Amen.

After asking your question and releasing any fear-blocks, your next step is to be extra-alert for answers that come to you. Since you are aware of your style of Divine communication, you'll look for a mental picture if you're visually inclined; you'll listen for an inner or outer voice if you are more auditory; you'll feel for an impression, a hunch, or an intuition if you are feeling-oriented; and you'll notice sudden ideas and understandings if you are intellectually inclined.

In the following chapters, we'll discuss specific steps to open each of the four channels of Divine communication fully. You'll also meet some of my clients, and learn how they discovered ways to distinguish true Divine guidance from the voice of their lower self.

CHAPTER SEVEN

⟨∞⟩

Making the Decision to Open the Channels of Divine Communication

Now that you are aware of your natural style of Divine communication, it's time to begin opening the channel or channels even further. You can also open the remaining channels of Divine communication. It's natural for us to be fully clairvoyant, clairaudient, clairsentient, and claircognizant. By taking steps that are described in the following chapters, you can open all four channels of Divine guidance even more, and you will have no difficulty in noticing, understanding, and following guidance from God and the angels.

The first step in opening the Divine communication channels further is by making the decision to have them open. This is a mental process that means you are willing to see, hear, feel, and know the guidance that God has for you. Through this intention, your experience of clearly receiving Divine guidance rapidly follows.

The reason it's important to start with this decision-making process is that, somewhere along the way, you decided to close your channels to Divine guidance. Like all children, you were born with the ability to receive information from heaven through all four clairs. The only reason adults don't clearly receive Divine guidance is that we chose to shut it off. Fortunately, we can choose to reestablish our link to the Divine.

The Intial Steps to Divine Communication

1. Be certain that you truly desire Divine guidance.

2. If you have fears or doubts, ask for heavenly assistance in healing them.

3. Become quiet within yourself.

4. Take a few deep breaths.

5. Ask the question for which you honestly desire an answer.

6. Let go; don't try to force an answer (or the answer you desire) to come to you.

7. Know your Divine communication style—visual, auditory, feeling, or knowingness—and pay careful attention to sudden images, messages, hunches, or ideas that come to you.

As Children, We Were Naturally Open

Perhaps you recall having clairvoyant experiences as a child. Many children report seeing angels and spirit guides, whom they or their parents call "invisible friends." In fact, Dr. William MacDonald of Ohio State University concluded from a 1995 study that children had a higher incidence of verifiable clairvoyant experiences than adults.[1]

If we all have innate clairvoyant skills, why do so many of us seemingly have difficulty seeing angels or our future? I've found that blocks to clairvoyance come from our decisions to shut off our spiritual sight. Here is a case study from my private practice to give you an example of this shutting-down process:

LIBBY

When Libby was seven years old, she had a spontaneous mental vision in which she saw her parents divorcing. In this vision, Libby saw herself and her mother moving out of the family home into a small, dark apartment. The vision showed Libby's father becoming estranged from her and the family.

Libby shook her head and screamed, "Noooo!" The vision frightened her. When it later came true and Libby's parents divorced, she secretly worried she had caused it with her vision. She made a conscious decision to never again have another vision. After that day, Libby had no more clairvoyant experiences.

By the time she came to see me for spiritual counseling, Libby was thirty years older and had forgotten the entire incident. Libby recovered the memory when she asked me for help in awakening her spiritual healing and Divine communication abilities. I asked Libby's angels for help, and they showed me the scene I've just described. As Libby recalled her childhood experience, she was amazed that her decision as a little girl could have followed her into adulthood. We then worked on releasing Libby's pent-up emotions.

Many young people purposely shut off their spiritual sight. The future they see frightens some, like Libby. Others feel afraid when they see angels or deceased loved ones. Some parents tell their children that spiritual visions are evil or wrong.

In my own case, my beloved mother was a talented spiritual healer who used clairsentience and clairaudience to contact God. Since her clairvoyance wasn't open, Mom didn't see spirits or angels. When I was a child and I told her that I saw transparent people everywhere, Mom told me that the spirits I saw were in my imagination. I thought, "Well, Mom is always right." I turned off my awareness that I could see the spirit world, until, as an adult, I decided to reopen my spiritual sight.

To counteract these childhood decisions, we need to release unexpressed emotions that surrounded our original choice to shut off our spiritual sight. This doesn't mean catharsis in the sense of screaming and hitting things. Rather, it means honestly facing the feelings we originally fled.

In Libby's case, she had to admit to herself how frightened and guilty she'd felt when her parents divorced. Libby also needed to release unforgiveness toward her father. Once she faced her feelings, Libby easily let them go. When her conscience was clear, Libby's spiritual vision automatically reopened.

MARCO

Another client, Marco, was scolded as a child when he accurately predicted his aunt's death. Marco's mother called her child's knowingness "the work of the devil," and locked him in his bedroom the day after his aunt's funeral. The next day, the preacher from the family's church paid Marco a visit. The preacher admonished Marco to stop speaking with the devil, lest his soul be lost forever.

Confused and frightened, Marco stopped talking about his knowingness. Whenever he had a Divinely inspired idea or knowingness, even a happy one, Marco purposely ignored it. Even-tually he lost all awareness of his knowingness.

When Marco went into business for himself, he became interested in reawakening his childhood claircognizance. After all, Marco reasoned, every knowingness he'd had as a child had proven true and trustworthy. He could really use this insight during his business meetings. Marco's adult religious convictions were not fear-based. He no longer believed or feared that his visions had come from the devil. "Besides," Marco told me, "if there is a devil, then I'll know if he ever speaks to me, since he supposedly always tells lies. My insights were always true, so there's no way they came from any dark side!"

I suspected that Marco carried a lot of contempt and judgment toward the religion and preacher of his childhood. During our spiritual counseling sessions, my suspicions were confirmed. When I explained to Marco that re-awakening his claircognizance required him to be free of judgments, as he had been as a child, he was willing to relinquish unforgiveness toward his church, mother, and preacher. Within one week of clearing his mind of harsh judgments, Marco reported receiving helpful spiritual insights and ideas.

Shutting Off Divine Guidance in Adulthood

Of course, not all decisions to close Divine guidance channels occur in childhood. Many of my clients willingly shut down their clairs as adults. Here are two examples:

LENORE

Lenore was a highly-paid executive assistant who worked for five managers in a health care corporation. Her job seemed to have all the perks: health and dental insurance, paid holidays, and a company retirement plan. The managers were very flexible when Lenore needed time-off to take her children to an appointment, or to pick them up from school. The only trouble was, Lenore couldn't stand her job.

She dreamed of opening her own home-based business. Over the years, she had developed a business plan, accumulated a hefty savings account, and come up with seemingly solid ideas for cultivating her market. Yet she was so frightened of trading in her secure paycheck for the insecurity of self-employment that she was virtually paralyzed.

Lenore came to me for help. She wanted to know what her angels said about the viability of her business. When, during the reading, I gave Lenore positive comments from her angels, she nodded. The angels were very clear that she, her customers, and her children would benefit if she started this new business. Lenore nodded again. She knew that's what her angels would tell me.

Yet she still wasn't ready to make the transition. In talking with Lenore further, I discovered one reason for her fears. Lenore explained that in all of her major life-decisions, she'd been able to "try on" each choice. She could then clearly feel how each decision would likely turn out, and make the choice that felt right.

"This time, I can't feel anything," she complained to me. Lenore actually had not felt any hunches for the past five or six years. I asked her if she thought it was a coincidence that this was the exact amount of time she'd been employed at her job.

We discovered Lenore had shut down her clairsentience as a protective mechanism. Since Lenore didn't want to face how desperately she desired to leave her job, it was easier to not face any feelings at all. She had unconsciously willed her clairsentience to stay closed so she could continue to lie to herself about her present unhappiness.

Reopening the channel to her Divine guidance took courage. She knew, instinctively that if she acknowledged the depth of her discontent with her job, she would end up quitting. Lenore had to prepare to face these circumstances before she was willing to reawaken her clairsentience. Once she was ready, and once she had lost the fear of losing control, Lenore's spiritual feelings resurfaced almost immediately.

Another of my clients, Catherine, shut off her spiritual hearing so she could engage in activities that she considered unethical and unhealthy:

CATHERINE

When Catherine first met her chiropractor, Dr. Ron, following her automobile accident, she thought he was extremely attractive. During their twice-weekly sessions, Catherine found herself becoming increasingly attracted to him. Perhaps it was his gentle touch, the way he relieved her back strain, or his friendly eyes. With every appointment, Dr. Ron spent more time talking with her. Soon he was discussing his marital problems with Catherine.

Catherine had always stayed away from married men, since Catherine's husband's affair had destroyed their own marriage. Catherine couldn't do that to another woman! She struggled with inner turmoil. On the one hand, she felt like a young girl with a puppy-love crush, anxiously awaiting her every chiropractic appointment. On the other hand, Catherine refused to face the fact that she and Dr. Ron were getting closer and closer to having an affair.

When Catherine saw me for an appointment during this time, we were scheduled to focus on spiritual counseling about her business. I had been seeing Catherine for several months, and had come to know her as highly spiritual and deeply connected to her Divine guidance. Still, during this session, Catherine's spiritual connections were obviously closed. When I asked Catherine to tell me what Divine guidance she'd received about her business, she reported getting frustratingly little.

I received a little nudge from the angels to ask Catherine about her chiropractic treatments. Although I didn't know why I was directed to ask about this topic, I trusted the angels, and I soon discovered that the topic was very related to Catherine's block in talking about her business.

Since my previous dealings with Catherine had taught me that she was primarily clairaudient, I asked her, "What guidance did you hear at the chiropractor that you didn't like, and caused you to shut off?"

Catherine gasped, then sighed. After a few minutes, she told me that she had clearly heard a warning that having a love affair with this married man would be emotionally painful. She had unconsciously willed that these words be removed from her awareness. That way, she could feign ignorance to herself while she drifted closer and closer to the affair. If she kept her clairaudience closed off, she would be deaf to its truth.

Unfortunately, when Catherine closed her main spiritual channel of communication about one area of her life, she closed it to all. During this time, when her business was increasingly successful, she very much needed her Divine guidance. So Catherine decided to face her ambiguous feelings about Dr. Ron. Once she had processed her feelings during our session, Catherine decided, on her own accord, to stop her chiropractic sessions. "I want to hear the truth again!" she said to God and her angels during our session. When I talked to Catherine the following month, she reported that her spiritual hearing had been completely restored.

I hope that no one will conclude from Catherine's story that she was being punished or her clairaudience was being withheld for moral reasons. Catherine had turned off her clairaudience simply because she did not want to face the truth that she was defying her *own* standards. That way, Catherine could fly closer and closer to the flame of an affair without taking responsibility for her actions. She effectively kept herself in denial by denying what she was hearing.

Deciding to Reopen Our Clairs

Many of us have knowingly or unconsciously shut down our clairs for preservation. Since everyone has an equal capacity to notice and understand Divine guidance, you can gauge whether you have shut down your own clairs. Ask yourself these questions:

1. *When I was a child, did I:*

   • *See angels, spirits, or visions?*

   • *Hear the loving voice of God or spiritual companions?*

   • *Feel when something was wrong or when something wonderful was impending?*

   • *Know things that it seemed only an adult would know?*

2. *If I did, and if I no longer receive these forms of Divine guidance, when did I shut them off?*

3. *What incident or incidents occurred around the time I stopped receiving Divine guidance?*

4. *Do I desire to have full Divine communication today, even if I can't recall ever having it in the past?*

5. *Am I willing to release the blocks to Divine guidance?*

Questions 1 through 3 will help trigger memories of instances when Divine guidance came to you naturally. If you answered "yes" to questions 4 and 5, you have the motivation to reawaken your latent spiritual communication skills. The desire for Divine guidance is the biggest factor in ensuring that you will have it. If, however, you're unsure whether you want to see, hear, feel, or know angels, spirits, or the truth about your present life or the future, then your spiritual channels will remain dormant. It's all up to you.

It may be helpful to "want to want" spiritual communication. A student in my spiritual class named Marty was not sure he really could handle seeing angels, since they reminded him of ghosts and other spooky things. Yet Marty really wished to desire spiritual sight. After all, his classmates were always oohing and ahhing about the beautiful angels they saw.

With Marty, we started working on his desire to want spiritual vision. This was all Marty needed, because his willingness to be open resulted in his being healed of the fear of seeing angels. "All of the angels and spirits are one with God and with me," Marty realized, taking a deep breath and smiling broadly. Marty understood that he'd viewed angels as separated from himself and from God.

From Marty's spiritual studies, he knew that whenever we view someone, even an angel, as a separated being, we automatically cloak ourselves in fear. When Marty shifted his perception, he lost his fear of seeing angels, and he soon joined with his classmates in reveling in the beautiful beings of light that encircled our classroom.

As these stories illustrate, we are in complete control of whether or not we notice our Divine guidance. Although God and the angels speak to us throughout the day, they never force us to be aware of or follow their guidance. We have the ability to turn Divine guidance on and off as easily as a light switch.

Just as we must decide to turn on a light before we take action to approach the switch and then flip it, so must we fully commit to noticing our Divine guidance. We can't be wishy-washy about the decision; we must *really desire* Divine guidance.

That means being fully open to what we might see, hear, feel, or know—being willing to face our fears, willing to trust that there is a higher power in the universe that knows more than we do. And that also means being open to the joy, security, and harmony that come from following Divine guidance.

If you still feel resistant to receiving Divine guidance, and yet something propels you to keep reading, please know this is a normal reaction. Opening to Divine guidance is like changing any other habit in your lifestyle, and it can take time, practice, and a period of adjustment. So please don't judge yourself if you feel conflicted about whether or not you want to open the channels of Divine communication.

If however, you feel drawn to keep exploring the information about Divine guidance, this is a sign that your true self is hungry for this reconnection with God and the angels. Follow this hunger; it will lead you home.

Chakras and Our Spiritual Senses

The windows that allow Divine guidance into our conscious awareness open and shut according to our decisions. We call these windows "chakras," and in the chapters that follow, we'll be engaging in exercises to clean and open them.

Each of your physical senses has an analogous spiritual sense. Just as you can see, hear, touch, taste, and smell the material world, so too can you see, hear, touch, taste, and smell the spiritual world. The spiritual senses give you insight and guidance about the material world. Your spiritual and physical senses work in beautiful concert with one another.

From the time we are babies, we learn about our physical senses. We're told, "These are your eyes; that's how you see. These are your ears . . ." and so on. What we're not usually taught in Western cultures is the source and use of our mind's eye, our inner ears, and our other spiritual senses. No wonder they are dormant and misunderstood.

The spiritual senses are our direct links to God's divine and omnipotent mind. The energy of God is the same energy within our spiritual senses. And just as we use our physical eyes for physical vision, so we use our mind's eye for spiritual vision. We also call this spiritual eye the "third eye," or the "brow chakra." We also have left and right ear chakras that are used for clairaudience, a heart chakra that is instrumental in clairsentience, and a crown chakra that regulates claircognizance.

The word "chakra" is from Sanskrit, the ancient language of India, and means "wheel." We have dozens of chakras within and around us. They look like spinning wheels, and remind me of whirling fans with blades overlapping one another.

Each chakra has a specific energy-regulation function. You have chakras related to each of your spiritual senses. The chakras glow in different colors, according to the speed at which they spin. The fast-spinning chakras have cool colors: shades of blue, green, and violet. The slower chakras have warm colors: red, orange, and yellow.

Clean chakras glow in pure and bright colors, but grow dim and muddy whenever we hold darkened thoughts such as anger or fear. For that reason, reawakening your spiritual communication channels usually involves chakra clearing. You can clear your chakras in many different ways. At my workshops, I conduct group meditations to clear residue from chakras. Chakra audiotapes, including my *Chakra Clearing* tape, are available at bookstores. In some of the later chapters of this book, you'll also read about powerful methods that I and my students have used to open the chakras so our Divine guidance is loud and clear.

Keeping a Divine Guidance Journal

Reading this book will stimulate an increased number of visions, sounds, feelings, and thoughts that are Divinely guided. I recommend keeping a Divine guidance journal where you record these occurrences. You can use any blank notebook to daily write brief notes about your experiences involving Divine guidance.

The value of this journal is that it builds your confidence in the accuracy of your Divine guidance. Once you realize that you accurately foresaw some future event—because it's written down in your journal—you'll be more likely to notice and follow your Divine guidance.

Most people also find when they keep a Divine guidance journal, the number of their spiritual or mystical experiences dramatically increases. It's as if the process of noticing Divine guidance creates more opportunities for it to occur.

Be sure to log in your Divine guidance journal such experiences as:

- *Premonitions.* Whenever you receive a vision, sound, feeling, or thought that pertains to the future, write it in your journal. Write about the way your premonition manifests for you later. You'll gain confidence in your visions, and also learn to decode your personal visual symbology. Premonitions also include things like knowing who is calling on the telephone before you answer it, or thinking about a person and then hearing from them that day.

- *Synchronicities.* When things seem to happen coincidentally, this is a sign that heaven is trying to communicate with us. Write down all events in this category in your journal.

- *Vivid dreams.* Some dreams are so powerful that we think about them all day long. These are often dreams that are Divinely directed. If you write the dream in your journal, you'll probably find it makes perfect sense to you later. Often you'll find that the dream warned you about something or foretold the future.

- *Receiving answers and information.* If you lose an item, and then ask God for help in locating it, write the experience in your journal. When you later find the object, notice the similarities between the location where the item was found and the impressions you received from Divine guidance. Keep a record of Divine information that comes to you spontaneously as well as in response to the questions you pose to God and the angels.

- *Mystical experiences.* These include miracle healings, seeing or hearing an angel or deceased loved one, witnessing an object moving on its own (such as a book that falls off the shelf just as you walk by), or having something materialize spontaneously.

CHAPTER EIGHT

⟨∞⟩

About Clairvoyance: Pictures of Guidance

By now, you have a clearer understanding of your personal style of Divine communication, and you've likely decided that you are ready to clearly receive your Divine guidance.

In this and the following two chapters, we'll look further at the first style of Divine guidance: clairvoyance. If you know you are primarily visual, or if you are somewhat visual, you'll learn how to become increasingly aware of your mental images. If you would like to become more visual, these chapters explain how to awaken this communication channel. You'll also learn how to have brighter, bigger, and clearer mental images.

With clear spiritual sight you can easily discern information about any matter that is important to you. You can see the future of your relationships and career. You can see the road conditions or weather before taking a trip. You can also see your Divine life purpose, and what steps you can take to fulfill it. The benefits of open clairvoyance are countless.

Please don't let the word "clairvoyance" intimidate or frighten you in any way. I realize that the term evokes images of a woman with big hoop earrings staring into a crystal ball. And crystal-gazing is certainly one form of clairvoyance. Yet, there are many other forms of clairvoyance that you've probably experienced, including dreams, mental pictures, movies, colors or auras, angel lights, visions, and symbols of clairvoyance that you've probably experienced, including:

Dreams

My mother had a vivid dream in which she played her violin. Mom hadn't played her violin in about fifteen years, and the last time she'd looked at it, the strings had been broken and the bow in disrepair. In her dream, the violin and bow were in perfect condition, and she played delightful melodies without effort.

On awakening, she went to the attic and opened her dusty violin case. There lay the violin and bow, in perfect condition, though she swore there had been a tangled mess of string the last time she looked! Mom took this as Divine guidance that she would benefit from playing music again. She immediately recommitted to playing the violin regularly. She loves the results of following this Divine guidance: the fun of participating in her community orchestra and the pleasure of playing beautiful music.

Snapshot Mental Pictures

Several years ago, I had prayed before going to bed. Several businesses that owed me money were quite delinquent. I asked God to help me resolve the problem and forgive the debtors. I asked Him for guidance on how I could receive the money.

On awakening the next morning, a picture quickly and clearly flashed in my mind's eye. There was a large, light-blue check with my name typewritten on it. The next day, I received the light-blue check in the mailbox exactly as I'd seen it in the mental snapshot!

Mental Movies

When my friend Robin had her first book published, she saw a mental movie of herself appearing on a major national talk show. Robin told me that this wasn't an intentional visualization to manifest a goal. In this spontaneous mental movie, she felt as if she were in an extremely realistic dream. She saw herself wearing a light-yellow suit, smiling and giving concise answers to the host's questions. Although Robin's publisher hadn't yet begun a publicity campaign for her book, my friend was certain that she would appear on this television program. So she carefully selected and purchased a beautiful light-yellow suit to wear on the show. Eight months later, Robin wore her new suit on the talk show, exactly as she had seen it in her mental movie.

Seeing Colors or Auras

Ever since Alain was a small boy growing up in Montreal, he remembers seeing colors around people. He knew intuitively that clear, bright colors signaled healthiness, while muted, dark colors meant the person was in transition or in crisis. At first, Alain assumed everyone could see the aural field. Only when he casually mentioned it to his mother and best friend did Alain understand that others were not clairvoyant.

Today, as an adult, Alain uses his aural vision to learn the integrity and character of his business clients. Whenever he sees red, black, or a sickly shade of green around a client, Alain knows to beware of the person's bad temper, substance abuse, or deceitfulness, respectively.

Angel Lights

Robert thought he was hallucinating the first time he saw a large flash of white light in front of his eyes. Had someone just taken a flashbulb picture? Was there a lightning storm? Did a lightbulb burn out? There were no lights nearby, so he dismissed it as a product of his imagination. When he saw white lights again two months later, Robert felt even more confused. This time, the lights were dimmer. They reminded him of the Fourth-of-July sparklers he would hold as a boy. When I explained to Robert that these lights are normal visual signals of the presence of angels, he felt relieved. "I thought I was going crazy!" he admitted to me.

Angel lights come in different varieties: large, bright flashes of light; soft, glowing trails of sparkles; and tiny flashes of white light. Usually the lights are white, green, or blue. White lights are from angels, and colored lights are from archangels. For instance, Archangel Michael has a bluish-purple glow, Raphael casts emerald-green light, Gabriel has a copper-colored glow, and Uriel shines a very pale shade of yellow.

Angel lights are a form of Divine guidance that reassure us we're not alone, but surrounded by loving angels. The peace that results from this realization helps us to be even more open to receiving Divine guidance.

Corner-of-the-Eye Visions

Ever since Janie can remember, she has always noticed people moving or standing to the side of her vision. When she turns her head to look, though, the people disappear. "Recently, my husband and I moved into his mother's home. She passed away last April. I swear that I see her out of the corner of my eye nearly every day," Janie told me. She explained that her mother-in-law was a wonderfully loving person when she was alive. "I feel like we have an angel living with us, so I'm not at all afraid when I see her," Janie added. "In fact, I find it comforting that she's watching over us and our home."

Visual Signs from Heaven

Rachel was devastated following her mother's sudden passing. She felt abandoned, lonely, and heartbroken. "How could God have let this happen?" she thought, furious. After all, her mother had done everything right. She'd volunteered, gone weekly to church, and had kind words for everyone. Now, she was gone. Life seemed so meaningless. In the weeks that followed, Rachel felt her faith in God's mercy fade. Yet she was not ready to become an atheist or an agnostic. In desperation, Rachel asked God to give her a sign. "Just let me know that You hear me, and that You are here," she prayed.

At that moment, Rachel saw a beautiful hawk land on her windowsill. Its feathers shimmered in the sunlight, and Rachel quivered as a strong chill gave her goose bumps. Then she decided, "That was too easy. Certainly, the bird isn't a sign." With this thought, she went for a walk. Twice, though, Rachel swore she saw the hawk follow her. The third time she saw the hawk, it sat on a tree branch and Rachel was sure it stared directly at her. When she returned home and found a large brown tail feather resting on her welcome mat, Rachel was convinced. The bird was her sign from heaven that God watched over and loved her. With this confirmation, Rachel felt able to heal her heart from grief and distrust of God's love.

Since Rachel is visually oriented, it was natural that she would see her confirmation of God's love in the form of a bird and feathers. In fact, birds and feathers frequently serves as visual confirmation of Divine guidance.

Symbols

As I worked with my new client, Trisha, I saw a mental image of a nurse's cap above her head. "You're a healer, aren't you?" I asked. It did not surprise me when Trisha answered, "Yes." I have found that Divine guidance helps me with clients by showing me symbolic pictures. When I work with clients who are healers, such as nurses, doctors, therapists, and students of the healing arts, I normally see this same nursing cap. I know it is symbolic because not all of these clients are nurses and nurses don't even wear caps anymore.

Common Visual Symbols and Their Usual Meanings
Symbols are a language all their own, and, much like dream symbols are rich with meaning. They are often deeply personal. In fact, they may have meaning only for you, like a secret language between you and your angels. Sometimes, though, we may not understand the symbolic meaning of a mental vision. If you see an image and don't understand it, ask your angels to help you. Say, "Please help me to understand what this means," and they will happily give you the information you need. God and the angels strongly want us to understand our Divine guidance. When we give them feedback such as "I don't quite know what you mean," they can better help us to understand their heavenly communications.

Although each symbol is highly personal, there are some universal themes within clairvoyant symbols. The following is a list of symbolic mental images you are likely to see, along with their common interpretative meanings:

Airplane—A trip is planned (usually means a trip to a distant place)

Angels (around a person)—This person is actively calling angels to his or her side

Baby—Pregnancy; approved adoption; positive new situation is on the horizon

Birthday cake with many lighted candles—A major birthday is coming up

Book—Divine guidance to read a certain book

Car—New car purchase; or use caution when driving

Candle, short and burning—Overexerting self; need to rest

City skyline—Person will be doing new business in and/or moving to a major city, such as New York or San Francisco (try to recognize the skyline in your vision, or ask your angels for additional information, which may come through one of your other channels of Divine communication)

Coffee—Divine guidance to cut down on caffeine consumption

Fire—Unexpressed anger

Food, plateful or bowlful—Divine guidance to avoid overeating

Horse—Freedom; running away from something

Mother Mary (standing over a person)—This person is especially fond of or works well with children

Nature scenes (such as a field of flowers, trees, or wild foliage)—Divine guidance to get outside in nature more often; also means that happy, carefree times are ahead

Plants, indoor—New growth in your life

Pregnancy—New birth or new venture

Road, bumpy—Challenges ahead

Road, forked—Choices ahead (count the number of forks in the road to know how many decisions will be faced)

Roses—Congratulations; happy news is forthcoming

Sleds or sleighs—A smooth ride or an easy transition ahead

Thumbs up—A go-ahead signal

Trophy—Success is either present or imminent

Typewriter—Someone with strong writing talents or aspirations

Vegetables—Divine guidance to eat more vegetables

Water, body of—Getting to know one's own self; the unconscious mind; becoming truthful with self

Water, glass or bottle of—Divine guidance to drink more water

You will likely see many symbols that will be uniquely yours. The angels use symbols in the way we use body language when playing charades. Imagine you were playing charades and you knew that a certain body movement would be particularly meaningful to one of your teammates. When the angels use a symbol that would be meaningful to only you and a handful of other people (as opposed to a more universally understood symbol), they are doing this out of their desire to help you. For instance, you may see scenes from your favorite movie because the angels know that you will understand their meaning more clearly this way.

Of course, often a visual image is literal, not symbolic. For instance, whenever I see a dog over a client's shoulder, I know this is a literal vision. It always means that I am seeing my client's beloved pet. I have to use a secondary channel of Divine communication to learn if the dog is living or deceased.

When in Doubt, Ask for Help

If in doubt, always ask your angels for clarification. For example, I had a recurrent mental image of a plateful of spaghetti that frequently appeared in sessions with many different clients. Clairaudiently, I would hear the phrase "spaghetti western" accompany this image. I was only vaguely familiar with this term, as I'm not much for cowboy movies. So I wasn't sure what the angels were trying to convey with this symbol.

By asking for the angels' help in clarifying its meaning, I eventually understood that the symbol meant a B movie with a contrived plot. Now, when I see spaghetti and hear "spaghetti western," I know I am dealing with a client who creates crises for him-or herself.

These clients, who are addicted to their own self-perpetuating dramas, are afraid that if they heal their minds and lives, they will be bored. As much as they feel pain from having, for example, unhealthful love lives or chronic financial problems, this pain seems normal and exciting to them. No one can heal when they are afraid of the consequences. Once they understand that peace of mind permits a rich and satisfying life, these clients are ready to let go of their roller-coaster lives.

When I teach my Divine Guidance classes, I notice that after students realize how many different forms of clairvoyance exist, they automatically begin having more clairvoyant experiences. It's as if this knowledge gives the subconscious permission to allow an increased flow of spiritual sight.

Enjoy the increased visions that will likely occur after reading this chapter. You may even experience some forms of clairvoyance that I didn't even mention. That's part of the fun and joy of receiving Divine guidance! God is eternally creative, and His guidance is always presented in newly creative ways.

CHAPTER NINE

❧

Seeing Clearly: Ways to Increase Your Clairvoyance

I've heard many people complain that they aren't visual. They say to me, "When I try to visualize something, I can't see anything." While some people aren't primarily visual, I believe we all have the capacity to increase the acuity of our spiritual sight. It's like building up a muscle, and simply requires a little exercise and practice.

As mentioned earlier, each of our physical senses has an analogous spiritual sense. These spiritual senses are regulated by the energy centers in and around our bodies known as chakras. Each chakra spins at a different speed and is colored differently. The third-eye chakra, which governs your spiritual sight, is dark blue with sparkles of purple and white.

You can do a simple meditation to clear and open your third-eye chakra. Here is one extremely powerful meditation, which usually results in the third eye either partially or fully opening right away. You can repeat the meditation as often as you like. With each meditation, your spiritual sight will grow markedly clearer. You may even want to tape-record this and the other chakra meditations that follow in this book, so you can close your eyes and listen while you clear your chakras.

Meditation to Open Your Spiritual Sight

1. Find a comfortable place to sit in a room where you won't be disturbed. Turn the telephone ringer off, and hang a Please Don't Disturb sign on your doorknob.

2. Envision that your room has filled with a beautiful, golden, metallic light. The light is from the angels, who are glowing, with this beautiful, light-filled, golden aura. Take two or three deep breaths of this golden light, and bring it into your lungs. Notice that as you breathe in the light, your body seems to feel rejuvenated and relaxed. Breathe in as much light as you can, and then slowly breathe it out.

3. Now bring your attention to the area between your two physical eyes. See or feel an oval object in front of you, between your two eyes. The object is lying on its side, and you notice that it is an eye—your third eye! This is the eye of your true self, the eye that records your entire life-history and will show you a review of your life when you cross to the other side.

See or feel if the eyelid on your third eye is open, partially open, or fully closed. If the eyelid is not open, take a very deep breath of the golden light. Bring the light inside your head. Now, with your breath and intention, bring the light through your third eye and out in the room. Feel a slight pressure in your third-eye region as it responds to the cleansing light passing through it. Continue sending golden light through your third eye as you breathe in and out.

4. As you clear your third eye, you can also release any thoughts that could block your spiritual vision. The angels stand by, ready to help you clear away limiting beliefs. All you need to do is be willing to clear these beliefs. The angels will do all the work for you.

With a few deep breaths, become willing to release to your angels any fears you may have about seeing the truth or your future. Become willing to release to your angels any fears you may have about seeing them. Become willing to release to your angels any fears you may have about being persecuted, criticized, or harmed by reawakening your spiritual vision. Become willing to forgive those, including yourself, who seemed to have harmed you in any time or any place for having spiritual vision.

5. With your firm decision and intention, open your third eye's eyelid. Please don't try too hard, or struggle or strain. Simply decide to open it, and allow it to open as naturally and easily as any other bodily movement that you decide for yourself. As you see it open, decide to anchor it open. You know that you can close it any time you wish.

6. Give thanks to the angels for their help in clearing your spiritual vision back to its true and natural state.

Toning Opens Your Third Eye

"Toning," also known as chanting, is another method that rapidly creates clairvoyance. In ancient Egypt, people said "Amon" or "Amen," the name of the sun god of Thebes, to make him appear. Amon or Amen was said to bring visions of the future to all who beheld him. So "Amen" was sometimes used as an invocation for clairvoyance.

The Egyptian high priests and high priestesses, though, knew that clairvoyance was not a gift from a pagan god, but an innate quality emanating from the third eye. The Egyptians concluded that chanting "Amen" opened the third eye because of its vibrations. However, the Egyptians found that the word "Aum" was an even more powerful chant for opening the third eye than "Amen."[1]

The high priests and high priestesses taught their students to carefully enunciate all three syllables of "Aum" as Ahh—Uuuu—Mmm. By chanting these ancient tones, you too, will feel the vibrations in your third-eye region. Try chanting it right now, either quietly or energetically. Either way, you'll notice how each syllable vibrates the area between your two physical eyes. You may even feel pressure or a painful sensation like a dull headache. Don't worry, though. These sensations merely show that your third eye's eyelid is like a rusty door that hasn't been used in a while.

If you chant "Aum" seven times each morning and seven times before going to bed each night, you will begin to receive clear visual images of Divine guidance within a week. Only if you still had fears about spiritual sight would clairvoyance fail to occur. In these cases, it's advisable to reread Chapter 7 to release your blockages.

Spiritual Vision Exercise 1

This is an ideal exercise to increase the strength and clarity of your visions.

1. Begin by looking at an object near you. Study the details of this object for about thirty seconds.

2. Then close your eyes and study the object in your mind's eye. Ask your mind to increase the brightness, detail, and size of your mental picture of the object. Try to turn the object around in your mind and look at it from different angles. Practice this exercise twice daily, and your visions' acuity will increase tremendously.

3. Start to notice the physical surroundings of places that you visit. Make yourself pay attention to ordinary sights, and you'll soon notice the richness and variety of visual treats around you. Pretend you are a novelist who is mentally cataloging the details of every scene in your book. By noting minutiae—the grocery-store clerk's facial expressions, the color and grain of fabric on the hotel lobby's sofa, the shade of yellow in the local florist's sunflower arrangement—you become more able to access details from your visual Divine guidance.

Heaven Will Help You

God and the angels want to help us open our spiritual vision. The archangel Raphael is particularly happy to help us reawaken our Divine sight if we ask for his assistance. Raphael oversees all angelic healing work and he is the supreme healer among angels. He can heal any emotional or physical malady, and, like all angels and archangels, he can help many people simultaneously. However, the angels and archangels cannot intervene in our lives, except in life-threatening situations, without our invitation. The law of free will says that we have the right to do things—even painful things—on our own and no angel can interfere with our decisions.

The angels love to help us, but this universal law usually keeps them on the sidelines where they watch us get into and out of trouble. They wait for any indication that we are open to heavenly help: a thought, a prayer, a cry for help is enough. Whenever we show openness to their help, the angels instantly come to our assistance. Our only task is to *remember* to ask for help. Many of us wait until the last moment before we turn to God and the angels for assistance.

Spiritual Vision Exercise 2

Here is a very effective way to receive archangel Raphael's help in opening your spiritual vision:

1. Take a few deep breaths and mentally say, "Archangel Raphael, please come to me now." He is with you before you finish the sentence. Angels can be with many people simultaneously, and Raphael can help everyone who calls on him.

2. Mentally ask Raphael to place his right hand on the area between your two eyes. He will transfer a beautiful, emerald-green healing light that looks like a glowing waterfall from his hand to your third eye. You may feel a tingling as he sends this healing energy to remove stubborn fears that keep you from spiritually seeing. Drink in as much of this light as you desire.

3. Afterward, please remember to thank Raphael for his help. Your joy and gratitude are the only payment he asks.

In the days to come, you will probably have many spontaneous visions. As mentioned in an earlier chapter, it's a good idea to record these visions in a journal. That way, you can see how accurate they are, and also look for patterns that will help you decode your personal symbology.

The angels ask me to leave you with one final suggestion: please don't try too hard to have visions. Whenever we force, struggle, or strain, we use our lower-self egos. As you'll recall, the ego is the antithesis of true Divine guidance. Easy does it is the rule for receiving a steady flow of communication from God and your angels. We don't need to push for Divine help. Pushing is rooted in the belief that God doesn't have time for us. Happily, the truth is that God and the angels attend to all of us simultaneously. We merely need to ask for assistance, and then notice the visions when they come.

◦◦◦

CHAPTER TEN

Experiencing Clairvoyance for Yourself

You can train your mind to be clairvoyant. With a little practice and a firm decision to see into your future, you will receive presentient visions and these visions will be clearly understandable and accurate as frequently or infrequently as you like. You have a great deal of control over your clairvoyant experiences.

When I say "control," of course, I don't mean you would force yourself to have visions. As you'll recall from the last chapter, straining blocks Divine communication. *Straining* to be clairvoyant is very different from *deciding* that you would like to receive heavenly guidance as mental pictures. In the former, you push because you don't really expect to receive it. In the latter, you simply enjoy your God-given gifts. The attitude behind your desire for visions is everything.

Practice and Experience Are the Best Teachers

If you wanted to be a skilled tennis player, you would use a similar approach. You would learn the basics and practice them. If, on the other hand, you tried to skip the basics or never practiced them, you'd rarely hit the tennis ball. Some people may be born tennis players or clairvoyants, but *anyone* can become proficient if they wish.

When teaching my Divine Guidance classes, I've found that experience is the best instructor. I can lecture for hours about how to receive Divine guidance, and I can talk endlessly about all the scientific studies that prove everyone has spiritual communication abilities. But until I ask my students to actually try it for themselves, they don't believe they have the skills. As a clairaudient, I can hear the students in my classes thinking, "Everybody else in this class but me can receive Divine guidance. I'm the one exception."

RICHARD

When clinical hypnotherapist Richard Neves, Ph.D., was in one of my Divine Guidance classes, he mentioned that he really didn't believe in angels. He liked the idea of angels, and enjoyed looking at angel pictures and statues. But since he'd never, to his knowledge, seen, heard, or interacted with angels, he had no reason to believe they really existed.

Then I asked the class members, including Richard, to pair up with other classmates. "Please face one another," I instructed. "Now, with your eyes either open or shut, please call for angels to surround your partner. You don't need to speak aloud to call the angels. Simply hold the thought that you would like angels to encircle your partner."

I saw many angels appear in the room and hover around the students, so I knew the class had followed my simple instructions. Then I said, "Please choose which partner will go first. Whoever is to go first, please ask the angels to give you a message that they would like you to convey to your partner. Mentally ask the angels, 'What would you like me to say to my partner?' Then say that message, exactly as you receive it from the angels. You may receive the angelic message as a feeling, a thought, an idea, a vision, or spoken words. However you receive the message, please deliver it without editing or interpretation. Then have the other partner do the same thing."

The room filled with the sound of students talking. I watched their animated faces glow with beautiful smiles. They were obviously enjoying being channels for the angels. I couldn't see Richard because he and his partner were in the back of the classroom. Instead, the glowing beauty of the students enjoying the angelic energy captivated me.

After everyone had received and delivered their angel messages, I asked the class for feedback. One by one, the students walked to the microphone at the front of the classroom. They excitedly discussed how much they had enjoyed the session. Most of the students admitted they had been skeptical about their prospects of connecting with the angels. Many students said that since they had been in a heightened state while talking with the angels, they couldn't remember the content of the messages.

Then I saw Richard walk from the back of the classroom to where I held the microphone. Richard looked wide-eyed and shaken, and his face was drained of color. "I saw angels," he said slowly, without expression, into the microphone. He explained that he had gone into the session expecting just another meditative exercise. Then he opened his eyes.

"There were two giant angels next to my partner," Richard said, obviously shaken by the experience. "The angels looked at me and said, 'Believe in us. Believe in us.' They said it twice, just like that, with a lot of firmness and love in their voice and demeanor. Although I had asked for a message from the angels to give to my partner, I know that the angels' message was directed at me."

Seeing is believing. After Richard's experience, he changed in two ways. First, he went from *liking* angels to *knowing* that they exist. Second, he gained confidence in his spiritual sight. The transcendence that accompanies clairvoyant experiences exceeds any verbal description. At best, words instruct you in how to see, and encourage you to try it for yourself. Until you try it for yourself, though, clairvoyance remains merely a possibility.

Clairvoyance Exercise 1
You can experience spiritual sight now, as you read this book.

1. Please take two or three very deep and slow breaths. There is a single-digit numeral in large type on a back page of this book. With another deep breath, allow your mind to see that number.

2. You may find it helpful to hold the book and ask your angels, "What single-digit number is printed in large type near the end of this book? Remember, don't try too hard or force yourself to see. It may be helpful to imagine that your mind's eye is a television set that you have just turned on. See the number slowly appear on the screen. If it seems fuzzy, then try to notice whether the number seems to have rounded or sharp edges.

Use your other Divine communication channels to enhance your clairvoyance. For instance, does the number *feel* like it's even or odd? Do you get a knowingness? Do you hear what number it is?

3. Release all self-imposed pressures, doubts, or fears of making a mistake. There is nothing to fear. Take another deep breath and ask again, "Please show me the number." Write the number you see, or, if you are unsure, write one or two impressions about what you believe the number is.

Then carefully turn to page 264 of this book, making sure you don't look at the other large figures that you'll use in other clairvoyant exercises in this chapter. After you find the number on page 264, compare it to the number you wrote down. If you saw the number that appears in the book, congratulations! If you wrote down a different number, please don't despair. It simply means that you were trying too hard, which is very common. In fact, the number or numbers you wrote down probably have similar characteristics to the number on page 264. Notice how many ways your number is similar to the book's number. For example, they are both even numbers, they have a similar rounded shape, they are very close numerically, and so on.

Clairvoyance Exercise 2

Let's try clairvoyance again. Take your time with each vision, and be sure to breathe! New students of clairvoyance often hold their breath while attempting to receive visions. This cuts off the source of inspiration that comes from your deep breaths. As you breathe in and out very deeply, ask God and the angels these questions. they want to help you to learn. Wait until you receive a visual answer to each question before proceeding to the next question.

Also, to avoid seeing the answers to the other questions, please wait until after you've written all five answers before turning to the back pages to compare your answers.

1. What is the large letter of the alphabet on page 265 in the back of this book?

2. What is the large shape that appears on page 266 in the back of this book?

3. What is the word that appears on page 267 in the back of this book?

4. Please show me the animal that appears on page 268 in the back of this book.

5. Please show me the scenario described on page 269 in the back of this book.

Clairvoyance Exercise 3

To increase your clairvoyant perceptions, practice receiving visions throughout the day.

1. Turn on the television to a program with which you are unfamiliar.

2. Then, either close your eyes or turn your back to the television screen. Listen to the television characters and your angels, "I would like to see in my mind what this person looks like." This is different from using your imagination to guess a person's height, weight, and build. Allow the visions to flow into your mind, and then open your eyes to compare your inner vision with the picture on the television screen.

This is exactly the method you can use to get a picture, ahead of time, of any person you are scheduled to meet. For instance, a high-powered businesswoman once asked to meet with me about doing some work with her corporation. Because I was a little nervous about the meeting, I asked God and the angels to give me some information about her ahead of time.

I took some deep breaths, relaxed, and asked God and the angels, "What do you want me to know about this woman?" Instantly, I saw a mental image of a friendly-looking woman with short black-and-grey hair. Once I saw this picture, I felt more peaceful about my upcoming meeting. After all, she looked very kind, gentle, and understanding. When I met her in person, I was pleased but not surprised that I instantly recognized the woman from my mental image. I felt very relaxed with her, and the meeting had a very positive atmosphere and outcome.

3. The next time you pick up a magazine, hold it and close your eyes. Take a deep breath, and ask to see a mental picture of the advertisement on the inside back cover. Again, don't force the images to come, and don't strain to guess what advertisement would be typical for the magazine. Just let it happen.

Very often, as I stated before, you will receive mental images related to the actual picture you are focused on. In one of my Divine Guidance classes, I asked the class to focus on receiving a mental picture of an advertisement I had at the podium. As the students took deep breaths and asked their angels to show them the picture, I stared at the advertisement and consciously broadcast this picture to the class.

The advertisement depicted a hugely exaggerated elephant stepping on a car. I don't recall what product this advertisement was trying to sell; I selected it because of its distinctive imagery.

Many students in the class received exact information about the advertisement. Other students saw symbolically related mental pictures. For example, one student saw a vision of India, which was related to the Indian elephant in the advertisement. Another student saw a beat-up automobile, similar to the car crunched by the elephant. Although not every student received detailed images identical to the advertisement, everyone got visions with some relevance to it.

With practice, you can discern which visions are literal and which are symbolically related. They have a different feel to them. The symbolic visions are useful. They gently guide you to see important messages that you might otherwise block out if you saw them literally. Sometimes our minds can accept only symbols instead of harsh reality.

Wording and Intention

Perhaps the most important part of receiving pictorial Divine guidance is in the wording and the intentions of the questions you wish to have answered. In other words, what do you want to see? God and the angels respond more to the underlying intention of our requests for Divine guidance than to our words. They see what we really mean, not just what we are saying. As *A Course in Miracles* beautifully says, "What you ask for you receive. But this refers to the prayer of the heart, not to the words you use in praying."[1]

So when asking for Divine guidance, focus on what is truly in your heart. If you have ambiguous feelings or confusion, openly admit them to yourself and God. Such feelings only become larger and darker if you ignore or deny them. Tell God exactly what you desire, and describe the different feelings associated with your desires. Since God already knows what is in your heart, this clarification and venting is entirely for your benefit. You are opening yourself to the light so it can chase away any shadows within you.

After ambiguity, confusion, and fear are released, your questions to God and the angels become focused and clear. Clear questions receive crystal clear answers. The clarity of your communication with the Divine spiritual realm, then, depends on how clear you are with your own self.

Steps in Formulating Your Question

1. Think of a question that you would like God to answer for you. Select an area of your life that would benefit from Divine direction.

2. Determine what type of guidance you would like, and try to put your request into a single question.

3. As you create the question, notice your physiological responses. Do you feel any tightness in your chest, stomach, forehead, jaw, or fist? Did your heart rate or breathing increase? Did you suddenly want to put this book away and do something else? All these signs of anxiety show there is ambiguity or confusion surrounding your question.

Take a moment to breathe deeply and tell yourself and God how you honestly feel. You don't need to—and it's probably advisable not to—analyze your fears or worries. Simply admit the emotions and then feel them lifted as you give them to God. You neither want, nor need these fears, so please hand them to your angels and God without reservation. They are like yesterday's newspaper: completely unnecessary clutter in your life.

After you admit one fear, you'll find there's usually another fear beneath it. As you release the feelings one by one, you will soon reach the core question for which you desire Divine guidance. You may also find, on reaching the core, that your answer is self-evident.

Since "clear" is the common prefix for all channels of Divine communication—clairvoyance (clear seeing), clairaudience (clear hearing), clairsentience (clear feeling), and claircognizance (clear knowing)—the clearer we are of fears, the clearer our questions are, and then the clearer the messages we receive.

One of the most profound and powerful visions I ever received was in response to my clear question to God, "How can I get closer to You?" I asked the question, with the full force of my feelings, while sitting at an Amtrak train depot. I had just finished reading a spiritual book that sparked my realization that I didn't feel as close to God as I desired. This realization evoked pain within my heart. I wanted the pain gone. I wanted God to hold me, comfort me, and be close to me. Intellectually, I realized that since God and I were one, I was eternally close to God in all ways. Yet I hungered for an emotional certainty that God was with me.

The instant I asked the question, I heard my train announced over the loudspeaker. I pushed open the depot doors to walk toward the train. That's when I received my visual Divine answer. I blinked disbelievingly as I looked at the people walking around the train. Everywhere I saw people glowing with the brightest, whitest light I had ever seen! I could barely see people's faces or bodies. The light obscured everything else. Although it was a dark, dusky afternoon, every person looked like a thousand-watt lightbulb to me.

I knew this vision was the answer to the question I had spoken from my mind and heart. The picture conveyed this truth: We feel close to God by seeing the spark of Divine light in everyone. Because I had been feeling detached from God, I'd seen only darkness in myself and others. God showed me another way of looking, and in so doing, helped me to recover a sense of closeness to His heavenly love.

Seeing the Divine Spark

You can use your new spiritual vision to see the Divine spark of light. With your inner vision, look for a small spark of white light in your or another's stomach area. It looks like a stove or furnace pilot light, though it may jump around like a shooting star.

People who have loving demeanors have larger "pilot lights" than those who hold unloving thoughts. But everyone has within them this light from the Creator. By noticing the lights in others, we stay reminded of the Divine light within ourselves.

Seeing the Angels

You can also learn to see the angels that surround every person you meet. Even the least spiritually-minded among us has two guardian angels by his or her side! An easy way to begin seeing angels is to work with a partner:

1. *Have this person stand next to a solid-colored wall.* It does not matter what color or shade the wall is, as long as its color is not interrupted by patterns or pictures. Room lighting doesn't matter either.

2. *Soften the focus of your physical eyes, and concentrate on the vision of your mind's eye.*

3. *Now, focus about two inches above the person's head.* Move your focus around the head and above the shoulders.

4. *Look for any instance of a white glow.* Don't allow your lower self to tell you that this is your imagination. Simply look for and notice a whitish aura surrounding your friend's head, neck, and shoulders. The pure white color is the guardian angels' glow.

The more angels next to a person, the stronger and brighter this glow will appear. Ask your friend to call more angels to his or her side mentally. Notice how the white light grows in size and intensity. You may also notice "angel lights" sparkling white, blue, or green as more angels throng to your friend's side.

By shifting your focus even further, you can actually see details of the angels' etheric bodies, clothes, and faces. This process is similar to going into a dark, crowded room. At first, you sense others' presences. Next, you see dim a outline. After adjusting your eyes, you see the other people in increasingly sharp detail.

Angels look very much like the traditional angelic portraits on Christmas cards and in Renaissance paintings. The angels can appear in any form, but they choose to appear in these traditional forms to help us recognize their presence. If we had a different conception of what an angel should look like, the angels would appear in that way. Their only motivation is to help us. So, as you adjust your eyes to see the angels, be assured that they help you along the way.

As you look at your friend and other people, first notice the white glow. Then, using your inner vision, look for a dim outline of an angel. As with our other clairvoyant exercises, please don't strain to see. Allow the visions to come to you, and you may be surprised to see several angels around your friend. The angels will likely be a variety of shapes and sizes. Some angels will be diminutive cherubs, while others will be magnificent archangels. You'll notice male, female, and androgynous angels. Many angels have small wings, and others have huge, eagle-like wingspans.

In the next three chapters, we'll focus on how to *hear* the angels and the voice of God.

CHAPTER ELEVEN

ॐ

About Clairaudience: Listening to the
Voice of Guidance

Perhaps you've had one of the following clairaudient experiences:

- You hear a song on the radio that seems to convey a message or a confirmation to you.

- A little inner voice helps you to make a decision.

- You happen to hear a snippet of someone's conversation, and the words are exactly what you need to hear.

- A loud voice booms from out of nowhere, warning you of impending danger.

The *Bible* calls clairaudience the "still, small voice within," and many times, this is a perfect description of the voice of God. But, the voice doesn't always sound small, and it isn't always within. "Clairaudience" or "clear hearing" comes from the heaven's broadcasting system in many different directions and amplitudes.

Clairaudience can range from a physical voice that seems to come from outside yourself to a voice that your hear inside your heart or head. Except when we are in danger, the voice can begin as a whisper. If we ignore Divine guidance long enough, God may even shout in our ear. Clairaudience always guides us in positive ways.

When Divine Guidance Is Shouted

During times of crisis or impending dangers, God and the angels use trumpeting voices to get our attention:

JIM

In January of 1996, Jim Clark was driving nearly 55 miles an hour down a Palm Springs highway when he noticed a stopped Lincoln Continental perpendicular to and directly in front of him. The Lincoln's driver, an elderly woman who was waiting to make a left-hand turn onto the other side of the highway, didn't see Jim headed toward her. It seemed inevitable that Jim would crash head-on into the driver's side of her car.

He stomped on the brakes and his car skidded and fishtailed. Suddenly, a loud voice screamed at Jim, "Let go of the wheel, NOW!" He obeyed, and took his hands off the steering wheel and his feet off the brakes.

Jim, who had never thought much about angels or spirituality before this incident, was amazed to see his steering wheel move on its own. He watched the brake pedal go up and down, as if it were a player piano being driven by an unseen force. The car miraculously went harmlessly around the back end of the Lincoln. A ten-foot deep ditch lay close to the edge of the highway, and Jim's angelic driver also steered clear of the ditch.

As Jim's car rounded the back end of the Lincoln, he looked in his rearview mirror. He saw a huge cloud of dust created as his car had exited the highway and driven around the other car. He saw that all traffic on the highway had stopped as the other drivers watched the near-accident. Yet Jim and the Lincoln were unscathed because he'd obeyed the angel's loud command to let go of the steering wheel.

The voice of the angel who warned of my car's theft was equally loud and to the point. Since I've been telling the story of my carjacking, many people have shared similar stories with me. As a woman named Mary shopped at a grocery store, a loud voice told her to leave the store immediately and go check on her car. Mary ignored the voice. When she was finished shopping, she discovered someone had stolen her car.

Divine guidance is loud and clear when we need to hear it. Sometimes God's voice becomes loud, after heaven realizes that we aren't listening to softer suggestions. Then the angels give loud and clear guidance to get through to us!

After I'd followed my Divine guidance to become a healer and author, I felt very satisfied. For some reason, I thought I was finished receiving Divine guidance, since I'd fulfilled every part of my vision. So I stopped checking in with God. That was a huge mistake. Without Divine guidance, I was like an airplane pilot without an air traffic controller to see what was ahead of me, behind me, and to the side of me. I tried to operate without knowing the full plan God and my higher self had in mind for me.

In this vacuum of Divine information, I began doing work that appealed more to my pocketbook and ego than to my true mission. I became a "love doctor," a frequent talk show guest expert and a magazine advice columnist on the topic of relationships. I told myself this was a helpful vocation, since people were genuinely hurt because of their love lives. Yet deep down, I knew I was betraying myself. I knew that being a love doctor was not my Divine purpose because *it brought me no joy.* I would see my name in the slick women's magazines above articles like "How to Tell if He's Mr. Right" and "How to Know if He's Cheating on You." I received no satisfaction or happiness from seeing those articles, or from seeing myself on the afternoon talk shows.

Still, I was making a lot of money as a love doctor, and I was reluctant to give up the steady income. The magazine editors and talk show producers pursued me, so I didn't have to worry about looking for love doctor work. It was plentifully available.

The angels had confronted me, as I described in Chapter 5, by asking me whether I planned to waste the life I had chosen for myself. The angels' explanation of how I had chosen my family for the lessons they would bring to me had affected me greatly. But it had not made a deep enough impression on me to cause me to change my lifestyle. I continued traveling to New York and Hollywood two or more times a month to appear on national television as a love doctor. And because my heart wasn't in my work, I felt tired a great deal of the time. So I drank lots of coffee throughout the day to energise myself artificially. Then, to turn off all that stimulation at night, I drank wine so I could sleep.

When the angels confronted me about wasting my life, I heard them as a soft and gentle voice accompanied by a very strong, palpable presence. I felt them surround me and hold my attention while they quietly counseled me about my life choices.

Since I'd ignored that quiet guidance, God apparently decided that I required a really loud voice if I were going to listen. I heard the same voice that would later warn me of the carjacking saying in a booming, staccato style, "Quit drinking and get into A Course in Miracles!" It was a firm but loving command rather than an angelic suggestion. This time, God had gotten my attention. I did research to discover what A Course in Miracles was. I thought it must be a class that you go take somewhere, but I found that it was a book, dictated by Jesus Christ as an antidote to the misconceptions about his biblical teachings.

It took six more months before I was ready to follow the Divine command. But when I finally did, I quit drinking and bought and began studying *A Course in Miracles* on the same day. As I soberly meditated on the *Course,* my life began healing. The *Course's* one-year meditation program, in the section called "Workbook for Students," helped me to tune into the still, small voice within.

My angels brought to my attention many life lessons that I could now hear and was more able to trust. One lesson they taught me soon after I quit drinking and began studying the *Course* was Live in integrity. I heard this wisdom deep within my mind and heart. The angels explained, in a very soft voice accompanied by loving feelings, that I needed to stop all behaviors that didn't mirror my highest image of myself.

I knew this meant giving up my steady income with the women's magazines and the talk shows. As much as I agreed with the angels, though, I wondered if they were out of touch with the real world. I thought, "Well, the angels don't worry about paying bills, so it's easy for them to tell me to turn down perfectly good money." Yet inside I knew they were calling me to walk in faith. I had to muster the courage to let go of the wrong jobs so I would create a vacuum for something better to come along.

The first time I said no to a magazine editor offering me a high-paying love doctor writing assignment, I felt elated. My feeling confirmed that the angels were right. I had to shed all of the behaviors that weren't serving my Divine mission. I had to sever a love-advice writing contract with one magazine, whose editor-in-chief hinted at a breach-of-contract lawsuit. I prayed a lot, as did many friends and family members. That magazine eventually replaced me with another columnist without bringing up the topic of lawsuits, and told me I was free to go. During this time, my income from my spiritually oriented seminars, articles, and books started to increase. By the time I let go of every love doctor activity, I had more money in the bank than ever!

True Divine guidance is repetitive and monotonous, as we discussed earlier. If you don't listen to or follow your Divine guidance, the angels and God will repeat it until you do. If you still don't understand their help, or if you choose to ignore it, God and the angels can become quite loud. This is especially true if you are praying for heaven to help you, yet are deaf to their answers. This is what I was doing: blatantly ignoring God's wisdom, while simultaneously begging God to help me. The only way He could get through the din in my mind was to scream, "Quit drinking and get into *A Course in Miracles*!" I'm surprised God didn't add, "for heaven's sake!"

In times of crisis, we can make it difficult for God to get through to us. He wants to comfort us and help us resolve the situation. Yet when we are frantic, we are unaware of all the help heaven offers to us. So God and the angels shout at us in order to penetrate the noise in our minds.

BRIAN

As Brian hurriedly dressed for work, he realized his wallet was missing. He searched the usual places: the bureau drawer, yesterday's pants, the bathroom, the kitchen table. No luck. Brian panicked.

He ran around his apartment, lifting pillows, papers, and other objects. Where was his wallet? He had to be at work soon, and needed his money and credit cards that day. Just as Brian walked back into his bedroom, a loud voice above his right ear yelled, "It's in your closet under your coat!" Brian shook his head. He'd never before heard a disembodied voice. Still, Brian was desperate, so he lifted his coat, which lay on the closet floor. There was his wallet, just as the voice had said!

The Still, Small Voice Can Be Lifesaving

Often, Divine guidance comes as a faint voice that, if we listen and follow it, can prove life-changing or even lifesaving. This is especially true if we're in a challenging situation and we're praying for God's assistance. He may answer us in a calm, quiet voice because from His perspective, He sees that everything is going to turn out okay. From our perspective, though, we may not be so filled with faith. If we become uptight during a crisis, we may miss out on hearing the Divine guidance that holds the key to unlock us from uncomfortable situations and crises.

RON

Ron Paul's car broke down at 2 A.M. in an area of Los Angeles that is considered very dangerous, especially after dark. Desperate, he got out of his car and flagged down a passing car. The men in the car agreed to take Ron to his home.

But after Ron had climbed into the back seat of the two-door car, he knew he was in trouble. The men began making derogatory comments, and said they were going to take Ron to a park. Ron knew that he was in danger of being beaten or killed, but he was trapped in the back seat with no exit door. He asked the men to let him out of the car, and they refused.

Ron began to fervently pray. He said to God, "You've always helped me before. I need your help right now!" At that moment, the car stopped at a red light. Suddenly, Ron heard an inner voice say to him, "Push the front seat forward and quickly climb out of the front passenger door." Ron obeyed the voice and was amazed that he was able to push the seat for-ward and escape.

The men in the car were yelling and driving after him. Just then, a city bus drove by. Ron flagged down the bus and the bus driver let him on. There were no passengers on board. Ron explained to the driver that he was in danger, and the driver offered to drive Ron home. The two men in the car chased the bus for a while and screamed at the driver to let Ron out of the bus. Eventually, the men in the car stopped chasing the bus, and Ron was driven home to safety.

The next day, Ron called the bus company to thank his rescuer. But when he asked to speak to the bus driver, he was told that no one by that name or description worked for the company. Ron gave the bus dispatcher more details about the driver, including the time and the street where the bus had picked him up. The dispatcher emphatically told Ron that they didn't have any buses that ran on that route, especially during the early morning hours.

Ron then realized that his clairaudience had Divinely guided him to be rescued by an angel who had miraculously manifested as a bus driver with a bus in order to save his life.

Hearing the Still, Small Voice

We can consciously decide to hear the quiet wisdom that comes from heaven as answers to our questions. This is just what my friend, Virginia, who sells metaphysical products to bookstores across the country, decided to do.

VIRGINIA

Virginia exudes the happy glow that comes from working in the field of your Divine life purpose. Virginia loves her work, and consequently she enjoys great success.

She recently had one challenge, though. Whenever Virginia called on the buyer for the country's largest metaphysical store, he was never in his office. Nor would he return Virginia's phone messages. As a metaphysically minded person, Virginia didn't waste time getting angry with the man. Instead, she wondered, "What am I doing to cause this situation?"

Virginia received a reply from her higher self's wisdom, "You don't really expect him to buy your products, so you call him at the wrong times." Hearing this answer, Virginia gulped as she recognized its truth. Deep down, she believed the man would reject her. Her negative expectations created a climate where she could not experience success with him.

So she first worked on healing her thoughts about the situation. As Virginia likes affirmations, everyday she affirmed and visualized her products sold in the man's metaphysical store. Virginia replaced negative with positive thoughts until she firmly knew she would succeed.

With her newly confident mindset, Virginia asked the angels to tell her when to telephone the man's office. Every day, she would ask her angels, "Should I call him now?" For three days, she heard a little voice say, "Now is not the right time. Wait a little longer." The voice was like a soft and gentle echo in Virginia's mind, barely audible unless her own thoughts were quiet.

On the fourth day, Virginia again asked the angels, "Should I call him now?" This time, the angels replied, "Yes. Call him right now." Without hesitating, Virginia dialed the man's telephone number. He answered the telephone immediately, and in a very friendly manner, invited her to his office. At their meeting, the man placed an even bigger order for Virginia's products than she'd hoped for. She told me, "Now I know that Divine timing means that I need to be willing to ask what the right timing is."

Virginia's story underscores the importance of being receptive to hearing Divine guidance. If she had been too defensive to hear the heavenly advice to change her expectations about having success with the man, Virginia would not have heard it. Many of my clients and students say, "I can't hear my inner voice," or "I don't know what God and the angels are trying to tell me" or even, "God never talks to me." Most of the time, they don't really *want* to hear Divine guidance.

Virginia also was willing to quiet the thoughts in her mind so she could be like a receptive satellite dish for Divine guidance. After all, mind chatter creates static and interference that competes for our attention when God speaks. Mother Teresa once said, "Before you speak, it is necessary for you to listen, for God speaks in the silence of the heart." Virginia was successful in receiving clear guidance because she pushed all other thoughts out of her mind. You too can do this, especially if you ask God and the angels to help you clear your mind. Remember, heaven can help you with *anything*, but first, you have to ask for help.

Sometimes, we're afraid of hearing Divine guidance because we don't trust its validity.

MARTHA

My client, Martha Naravette, was a high-school administrator who had come to me for spiritual healing of her back pain. Martha told me that she'd tried everything—physical therapy, chiropractic, Reiki, and herbology—but nothing seemed to work. Martha was on a medical leave from her job, and her insurance carrier required her to see a medical doctor specializing in back problems. The orthopedic surgeon had recommended immediate back surgery. That's when Martha came to see me for spiritual healing.

I could tell she was desperate. Although Martha didn't want back surgery, she wondered if it was the only solution since she wasn't finding relief any other way. I believe we create seemingly real experiences of physical illness and pain as delay tactics to block out Divine guidance. When we experience illness, we're too preoccupied with pain to hear the voice of God. So I frequently begin spiritual healing sessions by asking my client, "What has God been trying to tell you that you've been afraid to hear?"

My question usually takes clients by surprise, but it also triggers an honest reply. Martha took a deep breath. When she did, I heard her angels say that her back pain came from working at the wrong high school. The angels said that Martha wanted to move and work in a different area of the country to be nearer to her family. They also said Martha and her boss had frequent personality clashes. The angels wanted Martha to apply for work at the high school district near her family's home. However, they didn't want Martha to leave her present job until she'd made peace with her boss.

Although I'd heard the Divine guidance that Martha was afraid to acknowledge, I knew that it was best for her to tell me about it. If I told her, she might not believe its validity. But if I helped her to hear the voice of God and the angels, Martha was more apt to follow its wisdom.

"I . . . I don't know," Martha stammered. "I try to hear God's answers to my prayers, but I'm never really sure whether it's my imagination or not."

This is a common reply to my initial question. Yet everyone knows, deep down, what God is saying to them. Therefore, I always push a little until my clients acknowledge their Divine guidance to themselves and to me. So I used a different tack, "What is your back trying to tell you with its pain?" Martha faintly whispered, "It's saying, 'I'm afraid.'"

"And what are you afraid of?" I addressed the question to Martha's back.

With this question, Martha virtually *channeled* the Divine guidance that I'd heard from her angels moments before. Speaking in rapid and shallow breaths she explained, how frightened she was of leaving her present job. After all, what if she couldn't find another one? What if she were forced to take a lower-paying or less prestigious job? After she'd talked for twenty minutes, I asked Martha how her back felt. She was amazed to discover she'd been pain-free for for our entire session.

I taught Martha the same methods that are in this book so she could more easily hear and recognize her Divine guidance. She followed God's step-by-step guidance to apply for work at a school district near her family's home. Within three months, she was hired for a job even more prestigious and higher-paying than her former job. Today, her back is pain-free and Martha is no longer afraid to hear Divine guidance.

Divine guidance can help us with problems of any size, big or small. It's a mistake to believe that God helps us with only *major* life conflicts. God and the angels desire to guide us through every pitfall imaginable.

My friend, Richard, is a retired engineer. A near-death experience in his early twenties made Richard very aware of heaven's light and love. Still, his logical mind created doubts about God and the angels ... until he dropped his tape recorder in the toilet ...

RICHARD

Richard wanted to keep a dream journal, so he placed a pen and notepad on his nightstand. Invariably, though, he'd forget to write down his dreams in the morning. So his wife, Cathy, bought him a miniature, voice-activated tape recorder as a gift. It was a perfect solution. As soon as Richard awakened, he'd put the tape recorder in his front shirt-pocket and talk about his dreams into its microphone.

Two weeks after receiving the tape re-corder, Richard was finishing some household chores. While in the bathroom cleaning, he leaned over and was appalled as he watched the tape recorder fall from his shirt pocket into the toilet bowl. He fished it out and turned it on. But the gears didn't move, they just squealed. Pretty soon, the gears stopped too. The tape recorder had died!

Richard's technical judgment was that the water had shorted out the tape recorder and damaged it beyond repair. He was upset, and he worried about his wife's reaction to her broken gift. As Richard sat and looked at the tape recorder, wondering what he should do, an inner voice said, "Richard, take it outside and let the sun bake it." Richard smiled because the voice reminded him of the angel he'd met during his near-death experience. He asked if the voice was that of his guardian angel. The voice came back and immediately said, "Yes!"

Although skeptical, Richard obeyed the angel's guidance and took the tape recorder outside. The whole time he thought, "The tape recorder is ruined no matter what I do. It doesn't matter if it's dried out or not. It still won't work." Fortunately, Richard's doubts didn't affect the minor miracle orchestrated by his angel. After leaving the recorder in the sun, Richard went inside to call the store that had sold Cathy the tape recorder. They told Richard to come to the store in two hours, and they would have a replacement recorder ready for him.

Ninety minutes later, Richard retrieved his recorder from the sunny porch to take it to the store for an exchange. As he walked back into his house to get his car keys, Richard heard his guardian angel say, "Try it."

Richard's first thought was "Oh, sure!" Despite his skepticism, though, Richard pushed the tape recorder button and it worked! As he racked his mind to figure out how the shorted-out mechanism could have been repaired, Richard heard his angel say, "You're welcome!" Richard sat, stunned by what, to his engineering mind, was a true miracle. He looked at the tape recorder and said thank you to his angel.

When Clairaudience Combines with Other Channels

Sometimes, the sound of God's voice is accompanied by other channels of Divine communication, such as a vision, a feeling, or a knowingness. This was the case for Patrice Karst.

PATRICE

Patrice had always known that she was meant to serve a higher purpose in the world, but she didn't know its nature. So Patrice prayed fervently for God to show her what to do. At first, nothing happened: no sign, no word from God, nothing. Fortunately, Patrice never lost hope. She just kept praying.

Then, on a Saturday morning, Patrice suddenly awakened. As she opened her eyes, she saw the words "God Made Easy" in front of her. Simultaneously, Patrice heard a voice say the words to her. Patrice's immediate thought was "Wow, that would be a great title of a book. Maybe I'll write it someday." Patrice then closed her eyes to return to sleep.

But she couldn't sleep. A strong feeling told her, "Get up now and write the book." The feeling was unmistakably clear, and Patrice felt like it was a command, not a request. She crawled out of bed and grabbed a pen and paper. The same inner voice that had earlier said "God Made Easy" then dictated sentences that Patrice wrote on the paper. An hour later, she had twenty handwritten pages. The voice then announced, "This is to be a book and it will go all over the world, reintroducing the people of the planet to the wonder that is God." The following year, Warner Books published Patrice's inner dictation as the book *God Made Easy*.

When Another's Prayers Lead to Our Divine Guidance

We receive Divine guidance in response to life-threatening situations and to our prayerful requests for answers, suggestions, and directions. We also hear God's voice direct us in response to *other* people's prayers.

As I walked down a long flight of concrete steps to the Dana Point beach, I noticed a woman and two young children ahead of me. The woman, who appeared to be my age, was bald and wearing a cap. "Oh no," I thought, as I realized that she was seriously ill. At first, I attempted to insulate myself from thinking about or interacting with her. Then, my higher self took over and reminded me that there are no coincidences. Divine order had placed me immediately behind this woman on the steps for a reason.

I had recently received Divine guidance to work with people who have physical challenges. Yet, because of my Christian Science upbringing that said, don't think about sickness and you won't get sick, I had avoided interacting with physically ill people. I knew, though, the spiri-tual core of the situation: in truth, the woman wasn't sick at all, and I needed to keep my mind elevated above the physical plane when thinking about both of us. I claimed the truth that we were of one mind, and the body was just an illusion. Divine guidance told me that this woman was similar to someone exiting a building, because her soul was just exiting this physical plane, that's all. Nothing scary about that. She'd decided to check out and go home.

As I pondered this, an inner voice told me to talk with her. But how? I wondered, thinking it would be pretentious and ridiculous for me to run up and start a conversation. Just then, her daughter began to slow down. The young girl carried a large heavy, plastic bag and I asked her, "Do you need some help with that?" She shook her head and said, "No." Then a moment later she looked at me and said, "Well, on second thought, yes," and handed me the plastic trash bag, explaining that her inline skates were inside.

The little girl and I talked. She was Natalie, age twelve, from San Clemente. As we neared the beach, her mother, who hadn't noticed my presence, said to Natalie, "You doing okay with that bag?" in a beautiful English accent. Then she turned and noticed me with a look of surprise on her face. I introduced myself and consciously poured out love energy to the woman. Natalie decided she didn't want to ride her inline skates in the parking lot. They asked if Natalie could walk along the beach with me.

Of course, I agreed. As we walked, Natalie's speech was very animated about boys, school, and her stepfather. She wouldn't discuss her mother's apparent illness, and I didn't press the subject. We stood at the water's edge and Natalie taught me to skip rocks on the water. She had a strong arm and a man even came over to admire her pitching skills.

Standing at the water's edge, I taught Natalie to command a wave to stop when it threatened to roll accross our feet. "Stay! Stay!" I commanded the water, and it always stopped and rolled back to sea before touching our feet. At first, Natalie was skeptical. Then she tried it—and succeeded four out of five times. "See how powerful you are?" I told her.

"I'm not powerful at all," she demurred.

"You are *very* powerful, Natalie," I assured her. After that, Natalie successfully commanded the water to stop. I noticed that as I was encouraging another person, I lost all thought of my own worries and concerns. This was the gift of giving.

After Natalie rejoined her mother and little sister, I said my goodbyes and walked toward home. But the inner voice directed me to do one more thing before I left. "Here," I said to Natalie. "I'm going to give you one of my angels." I motioned for an angel that was over my right shoulder to come with me. Then I directed the angel to be on Natalie's left shoulder. "Her name is Priscilla and you can talk to her anytime. Anytime you want to talk to me, just tell Priscilla and she'll tell me."

"Where?" Natalie struggled to look at her left shoulder. "Where is she?"

"You can't see her, but you can feel her," I counseled. Perhaps Natalie *will* see Priscilla someday. If they talk together in the darkness as the girl relates her cares, hopes, and dreams to the angel, surely they will become the closest of friends.

Natalie said, "I'm sure glad you came up and started talking with us."

"Me, too," I said. Then I added, "I had a feeling you'd be nice!"

Natalie looked puzzled at my words. "Why *wouldn't* we be nice?" she asked.

Yes, indeed, I thought. Why would I expect anyone not to be nice? After all, the inner voice would never direct me to experience anything other than the nicest of situations.

Listening to Divine Guidance

The inner voice directs me to help strangers in various ways, and I have learned to trust its Divine guidance. I now rarely hesitate when God and the angels tell me, "Go give that homeless man some money," or "Say 'hello' to that woman over there." These experiences always end up enriching me as much, or more, than the people with whom I interact. I know, when I receive these Divine directives, that God is asking me to help Him to answer someone's prayers.

During my angel reading and spiritual healing sessions, I frequently receive clairaudient Divine guidance. I will sometimes hear it as a staccato sentence, such as "Forgive father," which lets me know that my client has unhealed resentment toward her father. I also hear detailed and elaborate words from God and the angels. I then act as a translator, giving my client the Divine guidance verbatim, without interspersing my own opinions or interpretations. This verbatim transmission ensures that my ego and interpretations won't interfere with the Divine guidance for my client.

Whenever we ask for heavenly help, we receive Divine guidance. It is the answer to our prayers. Our task, then, is to notice and then follow God's directions. Our human efforts, combined with God's omnipotent wisdom and creativity, create perfect solutions to every apparent problem. If we ignore Divine guidance, or feel afraid to follow it for any reason, we may assume our prayers are unanswered. Yet, *we* are the ones who aren't hearing. That's why opening our channels of Divine communication helps us to co-create with God.

I'm thankful that my spiritual ears were open when I received Divine guidance that helped me to find a new home several years ago:

At the time, I lived in a cramped and overpriced apartment near a tiny river. One morning, I woke up tired of apartment living. I was tired of paying rent, of my too-small bathroom and kitchen, and of the lack of water view from my window. I knew clearly what I wanted and I firmly asked God, without reservation, to deliver it to me. Probably because I was fed up with my current situation, my request for Divine guidance was to the point. I also had no doubts about what I asked for, which is surely the reason God immediately answered my prayer.

I said mentally, "I will not put up with this apartment any more. I want out now! I deserve and I ask to live in a home that I own, that is on a waterfront, and that costs less per month than my present rent payments. I also want it for no money down, since I haven't saved for a down payment."

A short time later, as I drove to work, a loud inner voice pointedly directed me, "Turn right on this street, now!" The command was so abrupt that I immediately turned my car onto the street. I had only driven a short way on the street in the past, but the voice told me to drive farther. I was partly concerned that I would be late for work, but I felt unable to turn the car around. The voice, combined with strong feelings, compelled me to keep driving until I reached an area that bordered a large, beautiful lake. There on the right was a condominium complex I had never seen before.

I pulled into the parking lot, charmed by the beauty of the blue, two-story Cape Cod condos. On a corner condo facing the lakes I saw a cute, geranium-laden windowsill with a huge hand-painted "For Sale" sign. My hands shook as I copied the telephone number from the sign, because I knew this would be my future home.

When I arrived at work, I called the telephone number. I could feel the presence of angels, with their palpable etheric hugs of assurance. I knew God was directing the situation, as everything effortlessly clicked into order: I immediately reached the condo's owner on the telephone and set up a viewing appointment for later that day.

When I met with the man, who was both a realtor and the owner of the condo unit, I discovered that he owned the place outright. The angels had two more happy surprises for me: the asking price of the condo was a fraction of what I'd expected, and the owner gladly agreed to my request for no money down. I had a signed contract and key in my hand one hour later. That weekend, I moved into the affordable waterfront home that I'd asked God to find for me.

So, the still, small voice within comes in many varieties. It can come as a commanding loud voice, or a firm-but-loving inner voice. We hear God's voice when we are in danger, when we need a little encouragement, or when another person needs our help.

Clairaudience from Music and Other People

God and the angels sometimes answer our prayers by giving us Divine guidance that comes from songs on the radio, overheard conversations, or chance remarks from another person.

CHERYL

A woman named Cheryl was devastated when her close friend Tony committed suicide. She grieved deeply, wondering if she could have possibly intervened and prevented his death. As Cheryl turned on her car's ignition the day after Tony died, the car radio was playing a song they both loved. Every day, Cheryl would hear this song in various locations: at the grocery store, when she was on hold on the telephone, and while she was driving.

At first, Cheryl thought it was just coincidence that she heard this song repeatedly following Tony's death. By the fourth or fifth day, Cheryl said aloud, "Okay, Tony, I get the message!" The musical message comforted Cheryl and helped her to heal from her grief.

We also sometimes receive clairaudient Divine guidance from other people, who deliver messages from God to us—often unknowingly.

JOHNATHAN

A man named Jonathan Robinson was contemplating traveling to India to meet the spiritual teacher, Sai Baba. The trip would be both time-consuming and expensive, and Jonathan felt indecisive. Finally, he prayed for Divine guidance to help him make the right decision.

Following his prayer, Jonathan felt strongly guided to turn on the television set. Although he normally didn't watch much television, Jonathan obeyed his inner command. Just then, a man on a television program said in a commanding voice, "You need to go to India!"

Jonathan knew that he had been Divinely guided to hear this message that, although part of a pre-taped television program, was the answer to his prayers. This message compelled Jonathan to travel to India, and he feels that this trip and meeting Sai Baba enriched him in ways that he could not otherwise have gained.

Our clairaudient guidance often comes through other people, as Jonathan's story illustrates. If we have faith that our prayers for Divine guidance are always answered, then we are naturally alert for the answers that come in unexpected ways. Faithlessness would have us write off such answers as coincidences. Yet, as Patrice Karst discovered, sometimes clairaudient Divine guidance comes from the mouths of babes. In this instance, Patrice could not explain her guidance as anything but Divinely given:

PATRICE

As Patrice drove her car one day, she felt de-pressed because it seemed that her life wasn't working well. Yes, she felt grateful for her six-year-old son, Elijah, who rode in the car's backseat. But everything else in her life seemed in complete disarray. Driving along, Patrice silently prayed for help, "God, I can't feel you right now and I'm frightened! My life is a mess and I can't feel your presence. Please let me just feel that you are here with me!"

A moment later, Elijah in an uncharacteristic, authoritative voice that almost sounded like a grown man, said enthusiastically, "Can you feel it? Can you feel it?"

"What?" Patrice asked.

"It's God! He's everywhere! He's in the wind. He's in the car. He's everywhere!"

Patrice's flesh was covered with goose bumps, because she knew that God had heard her silent prayer. God answered Patrice's request for Divine guidance by speaking through her receptive son, Elijah. Fortunately, Patrice was receptive to hearing this answer to her prayer.

Being aware and receptive is an important part of receiving, understanding, and benefiting from Divine guidance. In the next chapter, we'll discuss ways to increase the clarity and loudness of clairaudient Divine guidance, so it is understandable when you hear it.

CHAPTER TWELVE

⌒∞⌒

Hearing Clearly: Ways to Increase Your Clairaudience

Some people are naturally oriented toward hearing Divine voices. This is especially true if you are sensitive to noises, are musically inclined, or pay more attention to the sound of some-one's voice than to their actual words. Just as we use our phys-ical hearing to receive physical sounds, so do we use our spiritual hearing to receive Divine guidance that comes in words and sounds.

Everyone can become even more attuned to hearing Divine guidance. The two ways to increase the volume and clarity of your clairaudience are through releasing associated fears, and by practicing a few techniques.

Releasing Fears of Hearing Divine Guidance
Fear is the primary reason why someone can't easily hear the voice of God. God is everywhere, including inside us. So it's not as if we must strain to hear a faraway voice. The voice of God surrounds us and enfolds us. Our Creator continually speaks to us, and God's voice resonates from everywhere, inside and out-side us. The main reason we don't hear Divine guidance is we are afraid to hear it.

The fear of God's voice can stem from fears of being con-trolled. If you worry that God would take over your life or force you to do things against your will, you may resist by not hearing His voice in the first place. Or you may fear that God's guidance would make your life worse.

I certainly have wrestled with these fears myself. I remember feeling like a defiant teenager rebelling against authority figures whenever I purposely ignored God's guidance. I didn't want to be told what to do, even if it would lead to my happiness! I also remember fearing that God would make me give up the few material pleasures I enjoyed. I thought God's will was for us to live an aesthetically barren existence, devoid of all "human" joys. It took a long time for me to understand that only the lower-self ego wills for us to live miserable, barren lives. God's will is the same as our true selves' will: perfect peace and happiness.

Many of my clients and students, raised in fundamental religions, fear God's retribution. They avoid hearing Divine guidance because of assumptions that it'll be bad news. Like the dread of being called into the school principal's office, their guilt over perceived misdeeds creates fear that God will reprimand or punish them. Yet, this fear purely comes from projection. Since the lower-self ego is vengeful, but doesn't want to admit it, the ego sees this characteristic in everybody else— God included. In truth, God wills for us to correct our mistakes, not be punished for them. Since we are one with God, why would God want to punish Himself?

I help my clients feel comfortable with the "morality" of hearing Divine guidance by reminding them that it leads to increased joy, service to others, compassion, and love. These are all qualities of God, not the "devil". If anything, the lower self's guidance creates "evil" results such as depression, judgments, and addictions.

Sometimes, feelings of undeservingness stand in the way of hearing Divine guidance. If you feel that you don't deserve a happier job, a healthier love life, or a healthier body, then you will view all guidance toward that direction with trepidation. You would be afraid *even to hope* that your life could be better, fearful of being disappointed or of losing the new acquisitions.

God and the angels can lift these fears if you will allow them to help you. Simply take a few deep breaths and ask for them to help you release the fears that keep you from hearing Divine guidance. You don't need a formal invocation or prayer, just a sincere desire to be freed of the fears. As you request Divine assistance in releasing fears, you will feel and know that God and the angels surround you. When you open yourself up to help from heaven, you enjoy the relief that comes from shining light on any dark thoughts or feelings.

How to Clear Your Ear Chakras

Just like clairvoyance, clairaudience also improves when we clear its associated chakras. The *ear chakras* are directly inside the head near the left and the right physical ears. They rest at a thirty-degree angle pointing in toward the center of the head, and their energy frequency appears violet-red clairvoyantly.

The main source of ear chakra blocks is harbored fear or anger from words that you have heard. Anyone who has endured verbal abuse likely harbors fear or resentment in their ear chakras. These dark feelings lodge in the chakras waiting for us to mentally replay the hurtful verbal messages. We can let go of the old feelings so the ear chakras can clear, allowing for "clear hearing."

Nearly every weekend at my workshops, I guide audiences through the following method to clear the ear chakras. I then guide the audience to ask for Divine guidance and to listen for answers. People always come up to me afterward and say, "That was the first time I have ever heard the voice of an angel." or "Thank you for helping me to finally hear God's voice today."

Method for Clearing the Ear Chakras

1. Take two or three very deep breaths.

2. Visualize or sense your ear chakras by imagining two violet-red disks just inside your physical ears. See or feel these disks resting at a thirty-degree upward angle, pointing inward.

3. With another deep breath, mentally envision bright-white light cleansing the inside of your ear chakras. You can clean them simultaneously, or take turns cleaning the left and right ear chakras.

4. As the white light scrubs the chakras from the inside, mentally ask your angels to surround your head. Then, become willing to allow the angels to remove all the painful memories lodged in your ear chakras. You don't need to help the angels; just become willing to be helped. In fact, angels prefer that you don't *try* to help them, since our human efforts often get in their way. Instead, just be open to the angels' healing power as they cart away old feelings, thoughts, and memories that block you from hearing God's voice.

5. Ask the angels to lift any fears you may have about hearing Divine guidance. This includes the fear of being startled by a voice, the fear of being controlled by God, or the fear that you do not deserve God's time or attention.

6. With another deep breath, see or feel the angels illuminate your ear chakras with love and brilliantly bright light. We then say, "thank you" to the angels for their assistance.

After you've cleared your ear chakras and released your fears, you will experience a noticeable increase in clairaudient messages from heaven. Remember the characteristics that help you to distinguish true Divine guidance from the sound of your lower-self ego. True guidance, you'll recall, is always positive, uplifting, repetitive, and loving. The voice of the lower self is negative, critical, impulsive, and pessimistic.

The Importance of Openness

With your clear chakras, there remains only one block that could stall your success in hearing Divine guidance. This block occurs when you decide, in advance, what answer you want to hear from God. Very often, though we ask a question of God and the angels, we really don't want their help. We just want them to validate the answer that we have already chosen for ourselves. So we use our selective attention; if God gives us a different answer, we conveniently don't hear it.

Clairaudience involves being open to hearing an answer other than the one we desire. God's answers always bring happy endings, since His will for us is perfect joy. We may initially resist this Divine guidance because we have our own ideas of what the scripts of our life should be.

For example, let's say that you go into meditation and ask God, "How can I be happier at work?" Inside, you desperately want to hear, "Quit your job now and look for work elsewhere." Your preconception would likely cause you to miss the true Divine guidance that says, "It's not quite time yet to leave your present job. Love your co-workers and forgive your boss. First make peace at your current workplace, and *then* get your resume together to look for work elsewhere. By healing your current situation, you open the door for your next opportunity."

When we ask God a question, we must be open to hearing His creative solutions that may differ from our own. Since God is all-wisdom, all-intelligence, and all-creativity, it's wise to trust that heaven's perspective of our situation comes from a place that sees the entire picture.

I always think of God and the angels as if they were air traffic controllers who see where we've been, what's around us, and where we are headed. Asking for Divine guidance is similar to an airplane pilot checking in with the tower.

Music Increases Clairaudience

Playing soft classical background music in your home, office, and car increases the frequency and volume of your clairaudient experiences. More than one study has shown that soft background music increases the number of verifiable telepathic experiences.[1] Interestingly, many classical composers had spiritual backgrounds, including George Frederick Handel, who said that angels helped him write the famous "Hallelujah Chorus." Antonio Vivaldi, who composed "The Four Seasons Suite" was a priest who taught music lessons to orphans.

Music is very tied in with clairaudient Divine guidance. Many people have awoken to the sound of heavenly orchestral music, wafting from the ethers. The music is loud and beautiful, but brief. Perhaps it is the music of the heavens, which many near-death experiencers report hearing. In any case, the disembodied music is always a welcome sound, and is confirmation that the angels are near.

You can tune your spiritual ear to catch more instances of clairaudient Divine guidance by paying close attention to physical sounds. Listen closely to the subtle background noises that constantly surround you: man-made sounds, such as conversations and mechanical noises, and nature sounds such as wind, birds, and rain. Also notice, sound patterns in music, such as the bass trade and the rhythm. We often unconsciously tune these sounds out, just as we tune out the sound of the angels' voices. By focusing your ears on the subtle physical sounds, you more easily hear the subtle angelic voices.

∞

CHAPTER THIRTEEN

Experiencing Clairaudience for Yourself

Perhaps you have heard loud Divine voices yell warnings or advice. Maybe you've heard an inner voice gently guide you toward a healthier lifestyle. Or perhaps you're not sure whether you've *ever* heard the voice of God and the angels.

There is no one correct way to receive Divine guidance. If you regularly receive word from God through your feelings, knowingness, or vision, those avenues are just as efficient as hearing actual words. One channel of communication is not superior to another.

And while we all have natural inclinations toward one or more channels, you can fully open all the other communication channels. You will find that it's easier to understand what God is saying if you receive His messages through several channels. In that way, your Divine guidance gains detail and depth.

Clariaudience Exercise 1

On the following page, there is a list of questions to ask yourself mentally to elicit the experience of clairaudience.

1. Begin by relaxing. Take a few deep breaths and stretch your arms.

2. Say these statements and questions either mentally or aloud, addressing them to God and the angels. Please don't rush through these; take them one at a time, slowly. Don't strain to hear and don't guess at the answer. As you know, every time we push to receive Divine guidance, we close our spiritual senses. Clairaudience comes from relaxing into the moment and holding an optimistic expectation that God will answer you. Don't chase His wisdom; just ask and let it come to you. Remember, God and the angels want to help you learn.

- Please describe someone new that I'm going to meet in the near future.

- What new opportunity will soon enter my life?

- What changes do you advise me to make in my life right now?

3. After you ask yourself each question, close your eyes to shut out visual distractions. Then take a deep breath and listen. Listen for any words within your mind, or outside and above one of your ears. The words may or may not sound like your own voice. Usually, when Divine guidance comes from outside the head, it is positioned next to one ear. You will find that Divine guidance comes usually from one ear and false guidance from the other. The voice within, in contrast, seems to emanate from an internal speaker.

4. Write down everything you hear, even if the words don't make sense. They may make perfect sense in the near future, and you'll be glad you recorded them. Write the date next to each auditory transmission you receive.

You'll soon be able to compare your experiences with your clairaudient messages. As you notice the ways in which your clairaudient guidance was accurate, you'll gain confidence in your natural spiritual gift of prophecy. As you also see the areas where your clairaudience was off the mark, you'll learn how to distinguish true Divine guidance from false guidance.

Of course, it's also possible you received guidance that was accurate at that moment. But, because you have free will, you decided to alter the course of your future. In such cases, your clairaudience *was* accurate. Use your journal of clairaudient answers as a learning tool, and not as a test. Congratulate yourself on your successes, and learn from your inaccuracies. In this way, you guide yourself toward proficiency with Divine guidance.

If you still didn't hear anything, please don't allow yourself to become worried or tense. Instead, try again a little later. Perhaps you are tired, hungry, or distracted. If you do experience frustration or another negative emotion while working on this book's exercises, be sure to call your angels to you to clear these feelings away. Harboring negativity is a major block to hearing Divine guidance.

Most likely, though, you *did* hear a Divine voice. Now, your primary task will be to trust its validity. When first practicing clairaudience, it's normal to discount the voice as just your imagination. Recall the characteristics of true Divine guidance from Chapter 5 and compare these qualities with what you heard. Remember that the voice of the Divine is always loving and positive, even when it warns or confronts you. If you hear a scolding or insulting voice, this is the lower self's voice trying to frighten you. Simply tell this voice that you won't give it any power or air-time, and then ask God the questions again.

The lower-self ego tries to dissuade us from hearing and following clairaudient Divine guidance by whispering in our other ear, "What you heard is too good to be true. Don't believe it!" or "This is too weird. I can't handle spiritual communication: I want to stop!" The ego plays on our fears of being disappointed. The best way to deal with these thoughts and feelings is to surrender them to God. Tell God that you feel afraid, guarded, or frustrated, and then ask Him to handle the situation entirely for you. Don't hold back any negative emotions or thoughts; give them all to heaven. As you feel the release of negativity, know that you will soon feel more confident and experienced with Divine guidance. You *can* do it! We all can.

Clairaudience Exercise 2

Here are some more questions to give you the experience of hearing Divine communication. This time, the answers appear in the back pages of the book. After you ask the question, close your eyes and take some deep breaths. Continue asking the question in your mind several times and relax as you give yourself permission to hear the voice of God and the angels. Don't chase the answers to the questions; let them come to you.

- What kind of animal is pictured on page 270 in the back of this book?

- What word appears on page 271 in the back of this book?

- What is the topic of the sentence on page 272 in this book?

- What is the answer to the question on page 273 in this book?

After you have written all four answers, turn to pages 270 through 273, and notice the similarities between what you wrote and the images that are there. You will notice that some of your answers, although not exactly like the pictures and words in the book, share similar qualities. Or your answers may be symbols of the book's answers.

To build your confidence, focus on the similarities first. If you only look at the differences between your answers and those in the book, you may miss learning how to fully open your clairaudience. As with learning to ride a bicycle, have patience—and practice, practice, practice.

Experiencing Clairaudience for Yourself

Clairaudience Exercise 3

People who are clairaudient have a flair for automatic writing, a method of accessing guidance from God, the angels, and your higher self. The information flows through your hands and into your pen or keyboard. The words appear on paper or your computer screen, often without entering your mind first. My book, *Angel Therapy,* was written in this way.

Sometimes the hands have difficulty keeping up. If this happens, ask the spirit world to slow its pace a bit. There's never any reason to fear that this request would offend God or your angels. After all, it's their goal to communicate clearly with you.

The following exercise will allow you to write Divine guidance automatically:

1. Begin with a few deep breaths.

2. Say a prayer asking that only God and the angels come through your writing, such as:

P R A Y E R
TO ASK FOR ASSISTANCE THROUGH WRITING

Dearest God,

I ask to receive Your golden guidance through my writing. I ask that You and the angels watch over my writing, to ensure that all messages are from You and the angelic realm.

Thank You and Amen.

Of course, use any prayer that comes naturally to you, or use a familiar one such as the Lord's Prayer. In this way, you set the tone for your automatic writing session through your God-given intentions only to receive guidance from the Source.

3. After a brief meditation period, lightly hold either a pencil over a paper or your hands over a computer keyboard. If you choose the pencil-and-paper option, you'll want to use a steady writing surface.

4. Next, ask either a specific question, or an open-ended question like, "What do You want me to know?"

5. Words will come either inside or outside your mind. Usually, you'll hear a faint inner voice. This voice may be accompanied by a strong desire to write what you hear. You may even find that the pencil writes on its own. As you write the dictation onto your paper or keyboard, you will hear more words to write.

You may feel light-headed or a slight pressure around your head as you automatically write. It may dissipate as you become accustomed to receiving the high vibration frequencies of the verbal transmissions from God and the angels.

You'll be clearly able to recognize true Divine automatic writing by its tonal quality. Messages from heaven are loving, supportive, and positive. They ring true deep in your heart. Automatic writing from your lower-self ego, or from the egos of earthbound spirits, always rings hollow or false. These sources sometimes dictate frightening or even abusive material. If this ever happens, stop writing immediately and call on God and the angels to escort this source out of your consciousness and environment.

Automatic writing is a very safe and pleasant way for clairaudients to receive Divine guidance. The only exception would come from listening to and following false guidance. This exception is no different, though, than listening to false guidance that you received as a sound, a vision, a feeling, or a knowingness. As long as you listen to Divine Love, you are always protected and safe.

Clairaudience Exercise 4

You can also have powerful clairaudient experiences by working with a partner. Sometimes we can hear another person's

Divine guidance a little louder than we can hear our own. We aren't afraid to hear heaven-sent messages about changing jobs, healing relationships, and other disruptive or difficult subjects when they refer to someone else. In contrast, we are often very afraid to hear the truth about our own lives.

I teach this pairing-up procedure to students in my Divine Guidance classes. Every student that I've ever taught this method to receives messages from God and the angels. Some students receive detailed messages, while others receive fragmented or symbolic messages. Everyone reports enjoying this procedure, so I encourage you to try it for yourself. You will likely be amazed at the beautiful and accurate messages that the angels communicate to your partner through you.

1. Choose a partner who is open-minded and unafraid of receiving spiritual messages. A skeptical or fearful partner is difficult and unpleasant to work with.

2. Sit facing each another. Take a few deep breaths to relax. Choose which partner will go first in receiving and delivering the Divine messages.

3. Hold each other's two hands.

4. Close your eyes (both partners).

5. The partner who is receiving and delivering the Divine messages then mentally asks God and the angels, "What would You like me to know about (fill in your partner's name)?"

6. This partner should begin speaking when messages come into his or her mind. These messages may be words, thoughts, pictures, feelings, or a combination. Do not edit, censor, or try to interpret the messages. Just speak them to your partner as you receive them. The messages will probably make no sense to you, but they will make sense to your partner either now or later.

7. *Keep going. Deliver the Divine messages until you sense they are completed.*

8. *Take turns and have the other partner deliver Divine messages.*

By delivering Divine guidance, you are being an earth angel and helping God to spread His healing love and peace. With practice, you'll become more comfortable and proficient at giving angel readings. You may even turn it into an enjoyable new avocation or career as a messenger angel.

CHAPTER FOURTEEN

⌒∞⌒

About Clairsentience: Gut Feelings, Hunches, and
Spiritual Senses

At one time or another, many of us have said the following:
"I have a good feeling about this."
"I just have a hunch that we've driven too far."
"I get the feeling that something great is going to happen."
If you have ever had any of these experiences, you have
had a moment of clairsentience, or the reception of Divine
guidance through physical feelings and emotions.

We all have spiritual senses, so everyone has some degree
of clairsentience. Just as with the other clairs, you can learn to
strengthen your clairsentient abilities. Tuning in to this form of
Divine guidance is easier for intuitive and empathetic people,
who are usually very sensitive to the feelings of others.

The Many Faces of Clairsentience
Clairsentience can bring Divine guidance to us in many forms
and faces. It can manifest as:

- Tightened muscles in the stomach, hands, jaws, back,
  and forehead, as a sign of a negative situation.

- Butterflies in the stomach, as a signal of impending
  happy news; and sudden nausea in the stomach, as a
  sign of trouble.

- A hunch or a gut feeling to do something.

- A sinking sensation that tells you a situation isn't going to work out well.

- The feeling that a certain person is thinking about you, who later proves it by calling you on the phone.

- A strong, sudden emotion that's unrelated to your immediate surroundings, and later proves to be prophetic.

- A feeling of joy that tells you that you are on the right path.

- Feelings of peace that let you know everything is going to be okay.

- Smells that come to you from out of nowhere, such as orange blossoms signaling a forthcoming wedding.

- Feeling a sharp drop in room temperature, a sign that a person in the room has questionable integrity.

- Picking up on another's feelings as if they were your own emotions or physical sensations.

- Feeling a brush against your skin or a change in the air pressure, which lets you know that angels or deceased loved ones are around you.

Trusting Our Spiritual Feelings

With practice, you can learn to recognize and trust these signals. As discussed in previous chapters, acting on them is essential. Many people can recall times when they didn't act on their intuition and later regretted it.

Receiving clairsentience is just half the picture: trusting and following our gut feelings is the other. The willingness to

trust and follow clairsentience can make the difference between happiness and depression, financial security and insecurity, and health and physical challenges.

CATHY

When Cathy went to a job interview at a large brokerage
house, she felt her stomach tighten to the point of nausea.
The man interviewing her seemed pleasant enough, and the
job and salary sounded great. So why was her stomach tied
in knots?

From experience, Cathy recognized this sensation as a
warning of something negative. Nevertheless, when the inter-
viewer offered Cathy a high-paying position, she heard herself
accept.

The day after beginning work for the brokerage, Cathy
understood why she'd received the clairsentient Divine guidance.
She discovered that her three predecessors had quit because of the
harsh and stressful work environment. Within one month, Cathy
joined their ranks when she turned in her thirty-days notice.
"When will I ever learn to trust my gut feelings?" she asked me,
as she related this story following one of my workshops.

Like most clairsentients, Cathy will probably learn to trust
her feelings once an intensely negative or positive experience
has created a lasting impression.

GARY

A real-estate developer named Gary told me that he finally
learned to listen to his gut feelings following a very expensive
lesson. Gary and two partners had each invested $25,000 as a
down payment on a house in an exclusive beachfront housing
development. The partners planned to upgrade the house's
interior and resell it at a profit.

Right after escrow closed, though, Gary felt that something
wasn't right, although he couldn't put his finger on the nature
of the problem. He felt that something really bad would turn
his investment into a financial disaster.

The negative feeling was so strong that Gary decided to leave the project, even if he lost the $25,000. He shared his feelings with the other partners, but they persuaded Gary to stay. Gary also allowed his partners to talk him into investing more money.

Each partner invested an additional $250,000 to remodel the home. Since the other houses in the neighborhood consistently sold in the $2,000,000 range, the other two partners were certain they would make a tidy profit once the house sold. Gary wasn't so sure, but went along anyway.

Midway through the remodeling, the housing market in Southern California slumped. By 1991, when the house was finished, the market for high-priced homes had vanished. Despite their best efforts, the partners couldn't sell the house. A year later, they sold it at a loss just to escape the monthly mortgage payments. Gary learned a very expensive lesson to trust his gut feelings. Today, he always listens to and obeys his clairsentience.

I find that many clairsentients discount the power and accuracy of their intuition, until they've had several negative experiences from ignoring it. Eventually, they understand that these hunches and gut feelings are originating not from their imagination but from God Himself. When you realize that God speaks to you through physical and emotional feelings, you feel gratitude for these signals as they come to you. They are truly gifts from heaven.

Strong Emotions

Clairsentience foretells the future. Sometimes it comes as a sudden, strong emotion that's unrelated to your immediate surroundings. For example, an hour before your lunch break, you feel strong sensations of excitement and happy anticipation unwarranted by your normal schedule. During your lunch break, an attractive and interesting person talks to you, and the two of you make plans for a dinner date. The date goes wonderfully and is the beginning of a lasting love relationship.

Emotional Sensitivity

As you become more aware of your natural clairsentience, you are likely to become very sensitive to other people's emotions. This sensitivity is often called empathy. It means that you will feel what another person is experiencing when they undergo such joys as a victory or wedding. Empathy can be a profoundly moving and inspiring experience.

As your spiritual senses open and your empathic abilities strengthen, you may find yourself able to walk into a room and instantly discern the moods and emotions of the people there. Couples who have been together for years or have a strong emotional link report being able to pick up each others' feelings, whether two or two thousand miles apart. You may be able to tell when friends, family, or even strangers are in distress, and find yourself drawn to contact them at the exact instant when they need a helping hand.

Clairsentients are very sensitive to other people's emotions. Consequently, they often dislike crowds, as the intense energy can feel overwhelming. They also can absorb distress from negative people. Clairsentient massage therapists, for example, often soak up their clients' pain. And clairsentients who listen to their friends complain about all of their problems on the telephone often hear, "Wow, I feel so much better. I'm really glad to get that off my chest." Yes, but now the stress has been transferred to the clairsentient's chest!

The angels of my clairsentient clients have repeatedly given advice for handling these situations. First, the angels say that it is vital to hold a loving attitude toward the person with whom you are interacting. Avoid labeling that person as needy or dependent, or you will feel obligated to spend a lot of time rescuing them.

Instead, claim the spiritual truth about everyone with whom you talk with this affirmation: *This person, like me, is a holy child of God. God meets all of their needs. I will not view this person as dependent, sick, or broken. To do so would only hurt both of us, because we would create a negative reality from this negative labeling. Instead, I will see that God created everyone equally perfect. By seeing this perfection, I help the other person to see and experience their own Divinity in action.*

The angels say that they will help you with negative situations. They will guide you away from people whose consciousnesses are ego-based. If you do not follow their guidance and end up absorbing negative energy, the angels will help to clear you at your request. The angels also say that clairsentients should surround themselves with nature.

Here's what they told me to tell clairsentients about this topic: *We seek to shield you from absorbing others' pain. We will guide you past all situations that could rob you of your laughter and joy. Yet, if you seek our counsel when you have encountered another who has caused your mind to grieve, we will help you with our essence of healing love and light.*

We also counsel you to take Mother Nature's hand. Her plants, ferns, and flowers can shelter you from internal storms by taking up the darkness through their energy cells and roots. When, therefore, you have invited darkness into your presence, ask the nature angels among the plants to stand by and guard your energy from absorbing the dark.

The plants and the animals are your golden guardian angels who stand by to absorb that which is not from the light. Worry not that they will suffer, for they are instruments of the light, sent here for the very holy purpose of supporting your efforts to return home. The plants and the animals know to stand in the light of God's eternal love, and they rid themselves of darkness in this way.

Becoming more clairsentient is a double-edged sword. It can mean that you feel everyone's emotions, whether you want to or not. It's also a little like having a hearing aid that picks up all sounds equally loudly. Still, most clairsentients with whom I talk see their sensitivity as more of a gift than a curse. And it *is* a gift, a gift from God!

I often hear people discount their clairsentient guidance by saying, "Oh, it's just my feelings!" They act as if feelings are an inferior method of receiving guidance. Yet, our feelings are the route through which God and the angels often speak to us. Thank goodness that Jennifer Lulay Christiansen listened to her feelings:

JENNIFER

Jennifer has worked at a Portland business for five years. Every evening at the same time, she leaves work through the back door that faces the employee parking lot. Jennifer was accustomed to this routine, until one evening a strong gut feeling told her to leave work through the front door. She didn't question the feeling, but instead walked to the front door. But before exiting, another feeling told Jennifer to find a male employee to walk with her to the parking lot. Again, she obeyed her feelings without hesitation.

Jennifer and her male coworker walked outside together. But, before they reached the parking lot, a sharp popping sound filled the air. "Hit the deck!" screamed Jennifer's companion. "It's a gun!" They crawled back into the building, where Jennifer's companion, a war veteran, explained that he recognized gunfire only too well. Jennifer, on the other hand, had no idea what the popping sound was.

To her astonishment, Jennifer was told that an armed sniper was outside the rear door of her office building. If she hadn't obeyed her gut feelings and had walked out the back door, as was her custom, Jennifer would have been confronted by the gunman. Today, Jennifer regularly praises God and the angels for saving her life, and she also strongly counsels others to respect their gut feelings. "You never know when they could save your life," she says.

Because clairsentients are so connected with the feelings of their loved ones, they are also able to tune in to others' unspoken cries for help. Clairsentients can rescue others through the guidance they receive in their bodies and emotions.

As my friend Brenda drove to work one summer morning, she had an overwhelming feeling to return home. Brenda, who has learned to trust and obey her inner senses, immediately turned the car around. When she pulled into the driveway, Brenda understood why she'd been Divinely guided home. There on the porch was her fourteen-year-old daughter, locked out of the house.

Peaceful Feelings

Just as clairsentient feelings tell us when something is wrong, so too can they tell us when everything is going to work out well.

PAUL

Several years ago, I was in a car taking me to appear on a television show. The driver was a gentle and deeply spiritual man from Kenya named Paul. He told me that many Kenyan women, including his mother, give birth at home. Paul wanted to open a birthing center with a barter program where the women work in exchange for their health care. Paul was helping to put his brother through medical school, and later they would return to Kenya to open their clinic.

While driving along the freeway, we praised God and His heavenly plans for us. Then we smelled a burning odor, like smoldering rubber mixed with steam. It smelled too close to be from another car or a nearby factory. Paul pointed to the battery light and said, "Uh oh." He pulled to the side of the freeway and opened the hood. Nothing appeared wrong with the car, so we reentered the freeway. I said a prayer, and received in reply a strong gut feeling that everything would be okay. With this clairsentient confirmation, I relaxed because I had no doubt that the car would reach the television studio.

We drove for another hour without incident, except that Paul noticed his power steering wasn't working. As we neared the studio and idled in traffic, I saw steam coming from the hood. Still, the car was drivable and I arrived at the studio in time for the show.

The next day, I called Paul and asked him about the car. "It was a miracle we could drive at all," he said. He explained that after he'd dropped me off, he couldn't restart the car, and it had to be towed away. A belt had broken, and the radiator, battery, and power steering fluids had all drained out. "We certainly had an angel that made sure the car was still able to drive," he added.

Clairsentience As a Quiet Caretaker

Our Divine guidance reminds us we are never alone, being continuously surrounded by the love and care of God and the angels. We can ask for help whenever and wherever we are, and Divine guidance will *always* come to our assistance. A woman named Audrey experienced heaven's remarkable caretaking ability through her clairsentience.

AUDREY

Audrey is a vivacious European woman with a real zest for life. Her exuberance stems from her natural curiosity, which propels her to meet new people and travel to new places. Audrey has lived in five countries and speaks English, French, Spanish, and German fluently. She looks and says she feels at least fifteen years younger than her fifty-three years. Audrey probably owes her great health to her positive outlook and irrepressible curiosity.

Last year, Audrey suddenly had an excruciating pain in her lower stomach area. Doubled over, she worried what to do. She'd rarely been ill, and was not used to treating illness. Audrey was alone, and her family wouldn't be home for several hours. So she prayed.

"I suddenly had a clear feeling to take an extremely hot bath," Audrey told me. At first, she discounted this feeling as illogical. After all, Audrey normally showered rather than bathed. She also preferred lukewarm to hot water. Yet the clairsentient feeling persisted, and Audrey was desperate.

She crawled to the bathroom and poured hot water in the tub. As Audrey pulled herself into the water, she noticed her cramps were immediately alleviated. A while later, she felt well enough to walk from the bathroom to her bedroom, where she slept until her family returned home. Audrey awoke pain-free, and had no recurrences.

In the next chapter, we'll talk about ways to increase the clarity and frequency of clairsentient Divine guidance, so your intuition becomes more easily recognizable.

cᴐℐℴ

Feeling Clearly: Ways to Increase Your Clairsentience

Just as we use our physical senses for receiving physical and emotional feelings, we can use our spiritual senses to receive Divine guidance clairsentiently. Some people are naturally oriented toward picking up the kinds of messages that come as emotions, gut feelings, hunches, and intuitions. This is especially true if you are sensitive to emotions in yourself and others. Yet everyone can become even more attuned to receiving clairsentient Divine guidance.

You can increase the clarity of your intuitive feelings to more easily understand their meanings and messages. You can do this in a way that allows you to feel in control of the strength of your clairsentient signals, so you aren't overwhelmed with incoming energy.

Relaxation Increases Your Clairsentience

To receive clairsentient Divine guidance, begin by relaxing. Studies find that a person's physical comfort level affects their psychic abilities. Comfortable room temperatures, seating conditions, and clothing all increase the number of verifiable psychic experiences.[1] Since clairsentients are especially tuned in to sensory information, a comfortable setting increases your awareness and understanding of your true Divine guidance. I have found that having fragrant flowers, such as stargazers and tuberoses, in the room also enhances my clairsentience.

1. Find a comfortable and quiet place to sit during the exercise.

2. Take a few deep breaths and move your shoulders and neck around a bit to loosen any tight muscles. Adjust your seating position so you are completely at ease. The goal is for you to be so comfortable that your mind is not aware of your body, as any discomfort would distract your attention from Divine guidance.

3. Mentally call on the angels to surround you. Think, "Angels, please surround me now." You might visualize the angels circling you and the room.

4. Notice any feelings that follow: skin tingles, air pressure or temperature changes, warmth in your chest.

5. Think the words "Love, love, love," and sink into the feeling of being hugged by a giant cloud of unconditional love. Allow yourself to feel safe, protected, and loved.

6. In this state of sure protection and love, ask God and the angels a question. The topic of your question doesn't matter; they answer every question. The only criterion is that your question must be something about which you honestly desire Divine guidance. Go to the heart of your question, and mentally ask for answers and direction.

7. Be certain to keep breathing. To breathe or inspire means taking in spirit, or inspiration. If you hold your breath or have shallow breaths, you block Divine communication.

8. As you breathe deeply, notice any feelings in your body. Did you feel a tightening anywhere? If so, put your focus on that area, and mentally ask it, "What are you trying to tell me?" Be open to receiving an honest answer, because it *will* reply. You will only understand the answer, though, if your mind is open to receiving the truth. Then, have a mental conversation with that

part of your body that tightened or tingled after you requested Divine guidance.

9. Also notice the emotions that fluttered in answer to your question. Did
you receive joy? Feel its intended meaning, which is God's go-
ahead to improve your life. Did you feel a heaviness, a coldness,
or dread? These are warnings that you are headed off your path.

Heightening Your Awareness of Physical Feelings

Even when we're consciously unaware of receiving Divine
guidance, our bodies often acknowledge it with subtle muscu-
lar changes, such as tightening in the stomach, fluttering heart,
or perspiring palms. After becoming sensitized to physical feelings, you are more apt to notice clairsentient guidance.

Your awareness of clairsentient guidance will also increase
if you practice increasing your sensitivity to physical feelings.
You can try this right now:

*1. Become aware of your feet. Focus on how they feel. Are your feet
comfortable?* What is immediately next to the skin on your feet?
Socks, shoes, the floor? How does that feel against your feet?

2. Concentrate on your jaw, tongue, and mouth. Notice whether
your mouth is open or shut. Are any muscles in your jaw tense?
How about the other facial muscles?

*3. Notice any tension around your head, shoulders, arms, hands, back,
buttocks, legs, arms, and feet.* Think about tense rods of steel turning into limp pieces of rope. Did you feel your muscles relax
with this thought?

4. Notice how your clothing feels against your skin. What is comfortable and what feels uncomfortable about your attire?

*5. How comfortable is the surface on which you are sitting, standing,
or reclining?*

6. *Pick up any soft-edged object near you, such as a cup, napkin, pillow, or piece of clothing.* Close your eyes and slowly run the object across the skin of your hands, your arms, and the inside of your wrist. Focus your attention on the sensations. Try rubbing the object on one area of your arm, and compare the sensation to the feeling when you tap the object on your arm.

7. *Experiment with different objects and different pressures and motions.* The objective of this exercise is to increase your awareness of bodily feelings. The more you practice increasing your sensitivity and awareness, the easier you'll find it is to follow your clairsentient Divine guidance.

Opening Your Heart Chakra

Emotional feelings are also part of the clairsentient repertoire. The energy center or chakra corresponding to the emotions is in the heart and is known as the heart chakra. By meditating on the heart chakra, you can increase your receptivity to clairsentience.

The heart chakra becomes clogged, shrunken, and dirty from fears associated with love. Every person has suffered pain in some relationship, and this pain causes us to fear love. Yet because love is the essence of life, this fear causes us to lose touch with life's true essence. We become confused and forget what true love feels like. When we are afraid of love, we are literally afraid of being ourselves.

The fear of love leads us to become guarded, sarcastic, and defensive. We are so frightened of being hurt, manipulated, abused, or controlled that we seal our heart away from many experiences of receiving or giving love. Unfortunately, when we close our hearts to love, we also shut off the awareness of God speaking through our clairsentience. Ironically, this clairsentience reliably leads us to relationships that honor and support us. When we block the awareness of clairsentient Divine guidance, we are unaware of angels warnings about abusive relationships.

Instructions for Healing Meditation

Here is a powerful healing meditation to help you lose your fears about love and to cleanse your heart chakra. You may want to tape-record this meditation with soft background music, so you can easily listen to it once or twice a day.

1. With your eyes closed, and in a comfortable position, take two or three very deep, cleansing breaths.

2. Visualize a beautiful cloud of emerald-green light surrounding you. As you breathe in, you take this healing energy into your lungs, your cells, and your heart. Concentrate on your heart a moment, as you allow the emerald-green light to cleanse away any negativity that may have caused you to feel pain.

3. With a deep breath, be willing to allow the light to carry away any fears you may have about love. Be willing to release the fear of feeling love. You need do nothing else except breathe and hold the intention to heal yourself of the fear of love. Just be willing to be healed, and God and the angels will do everything else. Take another deep breath, as you become willing to release the fear of being loved, including the fear that if you are loved, you could be manipulated, tricked, used, abandoned, rejected, persecuted, or hurt. With another deep breath, allow all of these fears from any lifetime to be lifted and carried away.

4. Now, allow the light to cleanse you of any fears you may have about giving love. With a deep breath, be willing to release the fear that if you give love, you could be controlled, abused, deceived, betrayed, maimed, or hurt in any way. Allow all of these fears to be lifted completely, and feel your heart expanding to its natural loving state.

5. Allow yourself to release any old unforgiveness you may be harboring toward those who seem to have hurt you in a love relationship. Become willing to release unforgiveness toward your mother . . . toward your father . . . toward other parental figures . . . toward your siblings . . . toward your childhood friends . . . toward your adolescent friends . . . toward your first love . . . toward those whom you dated and loved . . . toward anyone you lived with or married. . . . Allow all of your hurts and disappointments associated with love to be cleansed and fully carried away. You don't want the hurt, you don't need it, and with another deep breath, it is lifted to the light where it is transmuted and purified. Only the lessons remain, and the pure essence of love contained within each relationship, since that is the only thing that was ever eternal and real within each of your relationships.

6. *Now, with another deep breath, allow the light to cleanse you completely.* Be willing to release any unforgiveness you may hold toward yourself connected to love. Be willing to forgive yourself for betraying yourself, for ignoring your intuition, or for not looking out for your highest interests. Give yourself a hug, either in your mind or with your arms. Reassure your inner self that you will never again engage in self-betrayal.

7. *You now commit to following your intuition and discernment, so you could never be or stay in any relationship that would hurt you.* Fully release the unforgiveness for any mistakes that you think you may have made in any relationship, including your relationship with yourself. And with another very deep cleansing breath, feel yourself healed, whole, and ready to enjoy the love that is the truth about who you really are.

As we lose the fear of love, we become more aware of the rich range of feelings that are part of our human experience. This is important, since detecting clairsentience's meaning requires an awareness of the spectrum of emotions.

Learning to Distinguish Various Feelings

Some people cannot distinguish or name the emotions that they feel. In such cases, it's important to increase the emotional vocabulary and learn how varied feelings can be.

An easy way to accomplish this is to use an emotional vocabulary list, such as the one on page 200. Make several photocopies of this list and keep them handy. Once or twice daily, stop and circle the feelings that describe your current emotional state. Within a week or two, this process will create a marked increase in your ability to distinguish one feeling from another. You will, for example, be better able to sort out your mixed feelings. This process also helps us to own our feelings and heal them ourselves instead of projecting them on other people, and then relying on them to change so we can feel better.

I used a list similar to the one on page 200 when I was in my early twenties and newly enrolled in college. I was just becoming aware of the variegated spectrum of emotions. In one of my psychology courses, the professor emphasized the importance of understanding your feelings. So, he regularly asked the students in the class, "What are you feeling right now?" When he'd ask me, I'd invariably answer, "Well, I think that I'm . . ."

The professor would interrupt and say, "No, Doreen. Don't tell me what you think. Tell me how you feel." When I answered, "Tired," he'd reply, "That's a physical feeling, not an emotion!" I realized I had very limited awareness of my range of emotions, so I used an emotional vocabulary list for several weeks. The rainbow of feelings I had inside amazed me! Through this process of discovery, I learned how to pinpoint the precise emotion I felt. In this way, I know the precise meaning of my clairsentient guidance.

How are you feeling right now? Circle all that apply:

EMOTIONAL VOCABULARY LIST

Adorable	*Comfortable*	*Giggly*	*Overwhelmed*
Afraid	*Concerned*	*Grief-stricken*	*Passionate*
Amorous	*Confident*	*Guarded*	*Peaceful*
Amused	*Criticized*	*Happy*	*Pleased*
Angelic	*Crushed*	*Hesitant*	*Polite*
Angry	*Cuddly*	*Hilarious*	*Quiet*
Annoyed	*Daring*	*Horrible*	*Ready*
Anxious	*Delighted*	*Interested*	*Relaxed*
Apathetic	*Demoralized*	*Irritable*	*Respectful*
Appreciative	*Disappointed*	*Jealous*	*Restless*
Apprehensive	*Eager*	*Joyful*	*Romantic*
Attractive	*Ecstatic*	*Kind*	*Sensible*
Beautiful	*Edgy*	*Lighthearted*	*Sentimental*
Betrayed	*Elated*	*Loving*	*Serene*
Blaming	*Emotional*	*Loyal*	*Serious*
Blessed	*Embarrassed*	*Moody*	*Sexy*
Blissful	*Entertained*	*Mushy*	*Shocked*
Bold	*Euphoric*	*Mysterious*	*Silly*
Bored	*Excited*	*Odd*	*Stressed*
Calm	*Explosive*	*Opinionated*	*Sweet*
Carefree	*Fearful*	*Optimistic*	*Tense*
Charming	*Fearless*	*Open*	*Ugly*
Cheerful	*Frisky*	*Offended*	*Upset*

You can use this vocabulary to decipher the intuitive guidance that comes to you. Whenever you feel a strong emotional or physical feeling, remember that it is a message to you. The feeling is the equivalent of a knock on the door. Our task is to open the door and listen to the feeling. One way to do this is by asking the feeling, "What are you trying to tell me?" Even if this process seems silly or feels forced, ask the question anyway. You *will* receive a reply.

Trusting Your Clairsentience

The next step is learning to trust the feelings. You may struggle with doubts over the validity of a clairsentient message. You worry that following the feeling's guidance may lead to hardship. Sometimes, clairsentients tell me they are waiting to receive "permission" from outside before allowing themselves to follow their gut feelings. Other clairsentients hesitate to follow an intimidating or seemingly illogical gut feeling.

One way to increase trust in your clairsentience is to review past occasions on which you were glad you followed your intuition, and occasions when you were sorry you didn't. You can also mentally "try on" a situation to feel what it would be like to follow your intuition and to know if you would enjoy the outcome. Another way is through repeatedly saying affirmations to reduce fear, such as, "I deserve happiness," "When I win, others win too," and "I fearlessly follow God's guidance for me now."

The best way to increase faith in your clairsentient guidance is to mentally ask God and the angels to help you release any blocks that keep you from enjoying full faith and clear feelings. Feel the release and lift as you surrender all fearful thoughts and energies to the Divine spiritual realm. You don't need to analyze your fears; just open your heart to God and the angels, and they will do all of the healing work for you. Repeat this method every time you feel afraid.

Occasionally I'll meet someone who is afraid of releasing fear. Recently, for example, a man approached me after one of my Divine Guidance workshops. He said, "I've now attended two of your workshops, and I have to tell you, this idea that you talk about, living fearlessly, is a frightening thought!" The man explained that he believed holding onto fear was useful. Since he'd suffered painful experiences in the past, he wanted to ensure they wouldn't happen again. He held onto fear to help him identify any new experience that reminded him of past hurts.

To this man, living fearlessly was the equivalent of being a babe in the woods: vulnerable, naive, exposed. After assuring him that I understood and honored his feelings and beliefs, I explained that I believed fear-free living was in fact the *safest* way to live.

"When our feelings are clear of fear, we are precise communication instruments linked to the infinite wisdom of God," I told him. "Fear is the equivalent of static on a telephone line that interferes with clear communication. God and the angels will warn you if danger is headed your way. But you may not hear their warnings if your telephone line is clogged with noisy fears from past events."

If you hold reservations about releasing your fears, you can begin with the premise that you are at least *willing to be willing* to release your fears. In other words, you'll consider becoming fear-free. And that little willingness is a big enough portal for Divine love to enter and heal you of fears that weigh you down.

DIANA

My Divine Guidance student, Diana, was afraid to experience her clairsentience. As a child-abuse survivor, Diana had endured extremely painful feelings that she had suppressed. She feared that awakening her clairsentience would open a floodgate of intense uncontrollable emotions. So Diana kept a tight lid on all of her feelings to stay in control.

During classes Diana attended, I talked extensively about the importance of forgiveness in clearing the mind, body, and emotions so they would be accurate receivers of Divine guidance. Diana told me that she felt her child abuse was "unforgivable," so she felt stuck with the anger and fear that accompany unhealed resentment.

"You don't need to forgive the act of abuse, Diana," I counseled her. "You only need to forgive the people involved: you, your mother, and your father. You are not *condoning* the abuse by forgiving. You are simply freeing yourself of the pain once and for all." We discussed her pattern of becoming involved with abusive boyfriends and an abusive marriage. "You can break this pattern by forgiving the abuse of your childhood."

I asked Diana to open a little window for heaven to help her, by being willing to forgive. "Don't try to forgive on your own. Just be willing to allow God and the angels to help you." With that suggestion, I watched Diana take a deep breath, close her eyes, and then shudder. We usually shudder when releasing old unforgiveness, so I knew that Diana was allowing God and the angels to help and heal her.

Afterward, Diana realized that she'd transferred her anger toward her father to God. "I was really angry with father figures, so it's no wonder I never talked to God," she explained. Once Diana decided to be freed of lower-self ego feelings, her clairsentience immediately awakened. Today, she is a successful spiritual counselor who helps other child-abuse survivors to heal their past hurts.

Remember that warm and loving feelings surround true Divine guidance, even when it warns of trouble or confronts you about unhealthy behaviors. False guidance creates cold, prickly feelings.

If you receive any guidance that makes you feel inadequate or afraid, then you are wise not to follow it. Instead, call on the angels and ask them to help you shed these feelings. Heaven wants to help you clear away the effects of the lower self's fears. They love to be called on to help you understand and follow God's glorious will for you.

When the late, great philosopher Joseph Campbell advised, "Follow your bliss," he meant we should ask for guidance; the joyful, God given directions are roadmaps to success in all ways. When you have joyless feelings, let them tell you what areas of your life aren't working. Ask God to help you have the courage to shed them, and to replace them with situations that truly make your heart sing.

Fears of loneliness, poverty, abandonment, criticism, and other pain come from the lower-self ego. It tries to tell us that, if we let go of joyless parts of our life, something terrible will happen. We must not believe the ego's threats, but instead, honor ourselves. If you feel resistance in any part of your life, listen to it. It is guidance from God and the angels telling you that something is amiss. Heaven does not will discomfort. God wills for you and all of His children to have your material needs met while you fulfill your Divine life-purpose.

God doesn't want you to do anything that could hurt you or your family. When you ask God for guidance, His power works through you to heal your life and the lives of those around you. You cannot fail, because God cannot fail.

In the next chapter, we'll go through some exercises to help you experience clairsentient feelings. This way, you'll get a "feel" for clairsentience.

CHAPTER SIXTEEN

cᗏᗌᕤ

Experiencing Clairsentience for Yourself

Clairsentience is the "force" that Luke Skywalker learned to master in the *Star Wars* movies. It is the invisible, inaudible energy that connects us with God, the angels, and other people. We can all tap into this force by paying close attention to our physical and emotional feelings, as in the exercises below:

Clairsentience Exercise 1

The questions and statements below will help you to experience clairsentient Divine guidance.

1. Read the following questions in a quiet, private environment. Address these questions to God and the angels, and then closely notice the physical and emotional reactions that you feel in response. Pause after reading each question. Then, you may want to take a few deep breaths and close your eyes to block out any visual distractions.

- What changes would you counsel me to make right now?

- What feeling from my past do I need to heal and let go of?

- Please tell me about my Divine life-mission, and what purpose I am supposed to fulfill.
- How can I experience more happiness in my life?

• How can I heal my (choose one at a time: financial, love, health, work) life?

2. Repeat the question in your mind and pay close attention to your physical and emotional responses. Clairsentience is nonverbal, so don't look for words that you hear or think. It's also nonvisual, so don't search for pictures in your mind's eye. Instead, focus on your heart and body.

As you asked each question, did any part of your body twitch or experience pain or pleasure? Notice any tightening, fluttering, warmth, coldness, joy, sadness, or other physical sensations. Let go of any judgments about your response, and simply allow the complete feeling to wash over you. Did you get a feeling about the meaning of this response? If so, "interview" your feelings to receive additional detailed Divine guidance. First, mentally ask your feeling, "What are you trying to tell me?" Then, open your awareness to the answer you feel in response to this question.

3. Write your responses to these questions in a journal. You can ask the questions daily for, say, seven days and watch how the clairsentient reactions become increasingly detailed over time. Remember that true Divine guidance is repetitive, so you can expect God and the angels to tell you the same answer every day. The answer usually becomes more detailed as you repeatedly ask a question. By writing the answers as they come, you'll be like a detective collecting clues that lead to your trustworthy deduction.

Clairsentience Exercise 2

This particular exercise will help you to gain confidence and trust in your clairsentience, and familiarize you with your personal language of feelings. I've always found that experience, such as this exercise, is the best teacher in helping us know and trust our channels of Divine guidance.

1. As before, ask the questions one at a time, and notice your physical and emotional reactions. Write down each reaction, and when you have finished with all of the questions, turn to pages 274 through 278 in the back of this book.

- What do I feel is the topic of the paragraph on page 274 in the back of this book?

- Do I feel that the single-digit number on page 275 has sharp edges or rounded edges?

- Do I feel that the word on page 276 in the back of this book is loving or unloving?

- What emotions do I feel when I think about the picture (without looking at it first) on page 277 of this book?

- What letter do I feel is portrayed on page 278?

2. After you've written your feelings in response to each question, look at the corresponding pages. Search for the many similarities your answers will have with what appears there, without allowing yourself to become perfectionistic. Perfectionism comes from fear, which is antithetical to the process of receiving Divine guidance. Remember, no one is judging you. Instead, focus on the similarities of the answers you received.

If you feel your answers were completely out of touch with what appears in the back pages, then try again later. It's likely you were distracted or feeling pressured when you first attempted the questions. Clairsentience, like any natural skill, improves with patient practice. The gift of clairsentient guidance is worth the effort.

When you try again later, use a magazine with which you aren't entirely familiar. Hold the magazine, close your eyes, and ask the angels to tell you about the advertisement on the magazine's inside back cover. Monitor your feelings and trust whatever comes to you. Then check the magazine, and notice the similarities between your feeling and the actual advertisement.

Practicing Makes Clairsentience More Powerful

You can also practice your clairsentience during everyday activities. For example, as you drive through a parking lot looking for an empty space, focus on your gut feelings. Allow them to direct your driving like a seeing-eye dog guiding you along. With trust you'll find an open parking space very quickly. You'll also gain confidence in your gut feelings.

In the same way, if you ever feel confused or lost while driving, ask God and the angels to give you directions. You will feel their guidance as either an urge to keep driving, or a strong feeling to turn in a certain direction. If you feel unsure of this Divine guidance, ask them to repeat it or to intensify the strength of the feeling. Heaven will gladly adjust and repeat the Divine guidance until you're absolutely certain of its meaning.

Another method is to focus on your feelings when the telephone rings. Ask yourself, "Is this a male or a female caller?" At a deep level, you will sense the feminine or masculine energy of the caller, and your clairsentience will give you an accurate answer. With practice, you can feel the specific identity of each caller.

You can also ask a friend to handwrite something on a piece of paper. Have your friend fold the paper before handing it to you so you cannot see the writing. Hold the paper in your hands, close your eyes, and take a few deep breaths. Ask your feelings, "What is written on this paper?" Notice your physical and emotional reactions to this question. You may get a detailed response that tells you the specific contents of the writing. Or you may get a feeling, such as happiness, sadness, warmth, or coldness. These reactions tell you the general *flavor* of the writing's contents. Then, open the paper and see what your clairsentience was trying to tell you.

Noticing your feelings is very different from *judging* or censoring your feelings. Noticing means we pay attention to, and then follow, the feelings as we would signs on a roadway. When we judge or censor, we argue with the road signs and ignore them.

Even if you're unsure of the validity of your feelings, you can easily train your mind to notice sudden emotions and physical sensations as they occur. Practice the habit of noticing these feelings and then asking them, "What are you trying to tell me?" Take a deep breath as you ask this question so you can have adequate silence in which to understand your feelings' replies.

Your emotions and physical feelings are messages from God, so in a sense, they are angels. It's important not to automatically brush off feelings, or assume that they are meaningless. They are very, very meaningful because nothing in this universe—and that includes your body and emotions—is accidental or coincidental.

You've probably had the experience of receiving an intuition and then talking yourself out of trusting its validity. Later, you regretted not listening to your intuition. Fortunately, we can turn these painful experiences into positive lessons that help us trust our gut feelings.

Each small success with clairsentience builds confidence, which in turn increases the amount of accurate Divine guidance received. Search for ways to practice your clairsentient abilities, and you'll soon know for sure that this force is always with you.

CHAPTER SEVENTEEN

ॐ

About Claircognizance: A Sure and Certain Knowingness

Claircognizance occurs when we receive Divine information as ideas, concepts, and thoughts. We don't hear, see, or feel this Divine information as it comes into our consciousness; it just suddenly appears. The Divine guidance is instantly accessible to us, much in the same way that data is accessible after it's loaded into a computer.

This process, claircognizance, or "clear knowing," is a little like having God put a computer disk into your mind. Information is loaded into your memory banks and is suddenly accessible to you. Though some people are naturally more oriented toward claircognizance than others, anyone can learn to increase their ability.

After all, our mind is joined with the mind of God. This means, in truth, that there is only one mind. This mind is all-knowing and completely creative and loving. We experience Divine guidance from this one mind when we "know" ideas that are profound and new to us.

Forms of Claircognizance

Claircognizance is different from brainstorming with yourself for ideas. With the former, you ask a question and receive an inflow of information. With the latter, you bat around a progression of ideas.

Claircognizance takes many forms, such as when you receive sudden:

- *Revelations.* Having a profound revelation, in which you know with certainty that you are one with God and all of life.

- *Aptitudes.* Knowing how to fix a broken item without looking at instructions and without being familiar with the item's construction.

- *Facts.* Someone asks you a question about a topic with which you are only vaguely familiar. Somehow, you find facts in your mind about the topic that prove to be accurate. You have no memory of ever learning, hearing, or reading about those facts.

- *Insights.* You suddenly know the bottom-line truth that lies beneath a seemingly complex situation. Your insight simplifies the situation by helping you focus on the core issue at hand.

- *Inspiration.* You find yourself writing or saying ideas and concepts that you had never thought about before.

- *Ingenuity.* You receive an idea about a new invention that is time-saving, lifesaving, or otherwise vitally needed in the world.

- *Foresight.* As you are introduced to a new person or situation, you know exactly the future course of this relationship or situation. You later find that your foresight is accurate.

Why We Mistrust Claircognizance

We seem to have the most difficulty in trusting this kind of Divine guidance. How can I know something, without knowing *how* I know?, we wonder.

Many people who are primarily claircognizant feel upset because the other channels of spiritual communication, seeing, hearing, and feeling, seem out of reach. This was the case for a woman named Yvonne.

YVONNE

I saw Yvonne as a client one day after I gave a speech at a Virginia Beach convention. Yvonne had requested a private angel reading, in which I relay Divine messages to clients. I arrived at her beautiful oceanfront room in the hotel where the convention was held. She asked questions about her career and family, which the angels joyfully answered through me.

While I give sessions, I try to encourage and teach my clients to receive messages on their own. As I talked with Yvonne, I realized that she was a claircognizant. Yvonne's frustration with her claircognizance was obvious when she blurted, "I never see any visions of my future like you and my friends do!" Many claircognizants feel ripped off because they cannot see mental images.

"My friends tell me just to shut my eyes and visualize," Yvonne continued, "but they don't understand that all I see is darkness when I close my eyes! I guess I'm not meant to receive Divine guidance." When I explained claircognizance to Yvonne, she noticeably relaxed. "That makes so much sense!" she said with visible relief. "I wish I'd known that I was a claircognizant years ago, because all this time I've been thinking there was something wrong with me!"

I explained to Yvonne that everyone can develop all four channels of Divine communication: visual, auditory, feeling, and knowing. Usually, however, we have one or two channels that are the strongest and feel the most natural. As a claircognizant, Yvonne can add clairvoyance to her repertoire though she'll most likely rely on Divine ideas, transferred to her from the mind of God, as her primary source of guidance.

Everywhere I go to teach classes about the four clairs, I meet people like Yvonne. Since claircognizants are generally intellectual people, they often feel confused by the illogical way they receive information. "How did I come to possess this knowledge?" claircognizants wonder. "I don't remember reading or seeing any programs about this topic. Where did the information come from?"

Many claircognizants keep these concerns a secret, fearful of losing credibility if others discovered their source of information. More often, though, claircognizants simply go through life frustrated because they can't understand how the information transfer occurs.

After learning about the four clairs, like Yvonne, they express relief at understanding how they know what they know.

For example, a technical writer told me that she couldn't figure out how she kept becoming privy to information about which she had no prior knowledge. A medical doctor told me that he always knows what a patient's diagnosis is soon after he meets the patient. "Yet the patients invariably won't accept my diagnosis, and I have to send out for costly lab tests, which always support my initial diagnosis," the doctor told me. He, too, conveyed relief at finally having a label for his experience of instant diagnosis: claircognizance.

Claircognizance is a sudden idea, concept, thought, or fact. It comes out of the blue, usually in response to a question you have mentally asked. Like all true Divine guidance, claircognizance is always proactive rather than destructive. The information comes to you in complete chunks, like a book that's been loaded into a computer's memory.

JANA

A woman named Jana Beals told me that as she read my book, *The Lightworker's Way,* she suddenly gasped. "Right then I had an instant realization: I just *knew* that I was going to meet you. I didn't know how I would meet you, since you live on the other side of the country from me. But I knew that somehow I was absolutely going to meet you! The following day, I received a flier in the mail that said you were coming to town to speak at a convention. I signed up to see you immediately." Jana told me her story when we met at the Florida convention three months later. She has allowed me to share it as a vivid example of receiving sudden claircognizant information.

People Who Are Primarily Claircognizant

Those who are primarily claircognizant are usually highly intellectual. They often hold jobs involving research, teaching, writing, and technical work. Many claircognizants are skeptics on spiritual or so-called paranormal topics, and most would vehemently deny ever hearing from God or the angels. Many would admit having difficulty believing in God and the angels. As I mentioned, claircognizants live with lots of doubts about *everything*.

Claircognizants are sometimes accused of being know-it-alls. Of course, this label is partially based in truth. Almost as if the collective unconscious poured information through a funnel and into the claircognizant's mind, this person receives guidance as complete chunks of information. You can ask a claircognizant a question on just about any topic, and they will give you a detailed and accurate answer. If you then ask the claircognizant, "How did you know that?" they usually shrug their shoulders and say, "I didn't know that I knew that until I said it."

People with other "clair" orientations may ask the claircognizant person, "*Why* are you doing such and such?" The claircognizant person will answer, "Because I know that this is what I'm supposed to do." If you ask, "But *why* do you know that?" or "*How* did you know that?" you will frustrate the claircognizant person. You will, instead, receive a reply such as, "I just know, that's all." And you will know that there is no arguing with a claircognizant who has a sure and certain knowingness.

The claircognizant person can be an engineer, a scientist, or a philosopher. He or she is usually good at solving problems, creating new ideas, and understanding abstract concepts. At times, though, this person's ego may weave additional information into received Divine guidance to create an extrapolated story that is only partially true. Consequently, claircognizants need to be especially aware of when they are operating out of their higher mind and when they have slipped into their ego mindset.

Claircognizants often enjoy philosophy and rhetoric. In every activity, no matter how ordinary, they search for underlying meanings and messages. They are also excellent judges of character. Frequently the claircognizant knows trivial details about new companions, such as their marital status, city of residence, or occupation.

CINDY

My counseling client, Cindy, told me that when she meets a new man, she knows in a flash the course of their relationship: what problems they, as a couple, will encounter; the highs and the lows of their love life. These Divinely inspired thoughts are always accurate, and Cindy is now learning to trust them before she enters new relationships.

I find that once claircognizants understand how their sudden ideas come from the omniscient mind of God, they lose their skepticism. At that point, they begin enjoying their spiritual gift.

KIRK & SANDY

Kirk and Sandy Moore were proud parents of two beautiful daughters. Their eldest, Tara, loved angels. As a young girl, Tara would hold open the car door so the angels could ride with her. At the dinner table, Tara insisted on having place settings and empty chairs available for the angels to dine with the family. As an adolescent, Tara read books about angels and sang songs about angels.

Then, at age seventeen, Tara was killed in an automobile crash. Sandy and Kirk were devastated as they drove home from the hospital. Then they noticed something on the kitchen sink they hadn't seen before: a cookie shaped like an angel! The Moores went to Tara's bedroom and there, in the middle of the floor, lay a piece of paper. As they picked it up, Sandy and Kirk gasped: it was the music for the song "You're an Angel." That's when they felt inner confirmations that their little girl was surrounded by her friends, the angels. Tara had become an angel herself!

Soon after, the Moores decided to quit their jobs and open a store devoted to angels: statues, stationery, books, clothing, and pictures. In a dream, Kirk received guidance about the location and the logistics of the store, which on awakening proved to be sound and accurate. They leased the shop space that Kirk saw in his dream, and Tara's Angels opened for business. Almost immediately, national media promoted their story and the Moores enjoyed great success. Kirk and Sandy knew that their angel, Tara, was in the background directing the store and the publicity.

When I met with the Moores one afternoon, I asked them about the communication channels through which they received Tara's messages. Kirk said he received Tara's communications visually and often heard her voice. As with most people, Kirk had more than one active channel of spiritual communication. His clairvoyance, combined with clairaudience, was especially strong in the dreams in which he interacted with Tara.

Sandy looked down and told me that she never saw and rarely heard Tara. She admitted feeling a little left out, as if Kirk and Tara had a special relationship that excluded her. I had a gut feeling that Sandy was claircognizant, so I asked Sandy, "Does Tara help you to run the store?"

"Of course!" Sandy instantly replied. "It's her store!"

I asked if she ever received information that was obviously from Tara's mind in her own mind. Sandy nodded her head vigorously and replied, "Yes, I do!"

I then explained to Sandy the process of claircognizance, in which we receive information, facts, or a knowingness from the Divine spiritual realm. We know, without knowing *how* we know. I said that some people, like Kirk, are visually oriented and receive clairvoyant spiritual communications. "And other people, like you, Sandy, are more oriented toward receiving intellectual or claircognizant communications from God, the angels, and deceased loved ones."

Sandy concurred, and told me how she was very aware when Tara guided her about which products to buy for the store. Sandy expressed relief to know that the absence of visual communications from Tara was quite normal. Like other claircognizants, clairsentients, and clairaudients, Sandy certainly can develop her clairvoyance through practice and desire. In the meantime, she can rest easy in the knowledge that she really is receiving steady communication from heaven through her claircognizance.

The Benefits of Developing Claircognizance

People who develop their claircognizance seem to have a slight advantage in receiving guidance that ultimately leads to business accomplishments. Most are very successful people. Although riddled with self-doubts about the source of their knowingness, many still put their heaven-sent ideas into action.

JONATHAN

Jonathan Robinson is a successful author, speaker, and therapist. As a longtime student of spirituality, Jonathan is in the habit of meditating daily. During one of his meditations, Jonathan asked God, "How can I serve people and have a good time doing it?" The thought of giving away ice cream on the beach popped into his mind.

Although the idea seemed unusual, Jonathan *knew* that it was true Divine guidance. So he immediately trusted it and took action. He bought twenty-five dollars worth of ice cream and headed to the local beach with a large sign that read "Free Ice Cream." Jonathan set up a little table with a large ice chest containing his frozen desserts, and braced himself for a rush of people coming to his ice cream stand.

But no one came. For fifteen minutes, Jonathan and his ice cream stand only received sideways glances from people. No one asked him for a free ice cream. Finally, a cute little six-year-old girl walked up and asked in a shy voice, "How much is your free ice cream?" Jonathan said that if she gave him a smile, she could have a double scoop for nothing. The girl laughed with delight. When watchful parents saw the little girl enjoying her free ice cream, other children and adults also approached Jonathan's stand.

As Jonathan scooped up smile after smile for wide-eyed kids, many of their parents asked why he was giving away ice cream. Jonathan explained, "I like to do nice things for people because it makes me feel good." As Jonathan scooped up ice cream for their kids, several parents asked what he did for a living. When he replied that he was a psychotherapist, four people asked Jonathan for his business card. In the end, three people he met that day called for appointments.

Months later, Jonathan totaled all the money he made from the appointments he had with these three people, and it exceeded $1,000. Jonathan concluded, "That's a pretty good reward for having a good time, making a lot of people happy, and spending only twenty-five dollars on ice cream!"

The Sure and Certain Guide

The sense of knowingness, once we learn to trust it, guides us unerringly. How do you learn to trust it? Most claircognizants gain faith in their knowingness through practical experience. When they don't follow their knowingness, they regret it. When they do act on their knowingness, they are glad.

My husband Michael, who is primarily claircognizant, has learned through trial and error to trust and obey his knowingness. A few months ago, for instance, he lost the locking lug nut from his car wheel. He looked all over the garage, but it was nowhere. While searching for the lug nut, Michael asked for guidance. He received a Divinely inspired thought that told him the lug nut was next to a speed bump by a road near our home. Michael walked right to the speed bump, and there was his lug nut!

Claircognizants also gain faith in their knowingness through recognizing the characteristics of true Divine guidance. Its repetitive, consistent, and positive content distinguishes it from the haphazard and demeaning thoughts from the lower-self ego.

Finally, though it may seem illogical, please remember to ask God and the angels to help you increase your trust in Divine guidance. Even if it seems silly or forced, ask them to clear away blocks that keep you from enjoying your God-given ideas. Even the most skeptical pragmatist will find that this method creates a powerfully impressive experience. An easy way to do this is right before going to sleep at night, say this prayer mentally or aloud:

P R A Y E R

TO CLEAR AWAY BLOCKS

Dearest God,

I ask You to enter my dreams tonight and clear away the fears
that keep me from understanding, trusting, and following Divine
guidance. If there is a message You wish to give me, please help
me to understand clearly and remember it in the morning.

Thank You and Amen.

Heaven will replace your distrust with faith, and you'll feel more confident about following your knowingness. With the methods outlined in the following chapter, you can increase the frequency and clarity of your heaven-sent ideas, even if you don't normally receive claircognizant guidance.

࿊

CHAPTER EIGHTEEN

Knowing Clearly: Ways to Increase Your Claircognizance

Inventiveness, accurate insights into people, and successful business ideas are among the benefits of claircognizance, as discussed in the previous chapter. In this chapter, we'll look at ways to open up the channel of claircognizance. If you are already primarily claircognizant, this chapter will help you to become more aware and trusting of this channel of Divine guidance. If you already favor another clair, you will learn how to strengthen your claircognizance.

Claircognizance and a Balanced Lifestyle

To increase your awareness of claircognizant Divine guidance, it's important to maintain a balanced lifestyle. I've found that taking good care of the body and emotions has an enormous effect on our access to Divine wisdom. Probably because of their intellectual orientation, people who are primarily claircognizant tend to stay holed up in their offices. I encourage them to balance their lives by spending time alone in nature, eating a nutritious diet, and getting fresh air and exercise. In fact, you'll probably receive your most important claircognizant ideas while getting fresh air and exercise!

A well-tuned body acts like a precisely calibrated instrument that can detect subtle variations in data. A neglected body, in contrast, is dulled to the exquisite nuances in God-given ideas. An inactive person with a poor diet usually misses the details of Divine guidance. Therefore, your physical fitness regimen has extremely practical applications. It is not a waste of time or a symbol of vanity, but an investment that will help you.

Increasing Your Mind's Receptivity

Clearing the mind of judgments is essential to receive clear, detailed claircognizant thoughts. It's the equivalent of unloading unnecessary files from your computer memory. Judgments are merely opinions, and you want to save room for the facts to come into your mind. A mind cluttered with judgments is usually too distracted to notice new ideas as they enter.

One reason why judging interferes with receiving claircognizant information is that judgments are affirmations that you and other people are different. This is a thought that leads to the conclusion, "I am separate from other people and from God." And you may recall, from previous chapters, that only the lower-self ego says this. When we're in our ego-mind, we cut ourselves off from our higher self, who is one with God. Staying centered in our higher self gives us access to the infinite mind of our Creator. You might say, that our lower self's operating system cannot read information from the Divine data banks.

There's a big difference, though, between judgment and discernment. Judging means putting qualitative labels, like "good" or "bad" onto people, objects, or situations. These labels put blinders on our minds, box-in our thinking, and deaden our creative abilities. Discernment, in contrast, is the process of allowing Divine guidance to steer us toward or away from people, objects, and situations. We allow our higher self, God, and the angels to decide which relationship, possessions, and careers would bring the greatest joy to us and the world. For example, instead of saying to ourselves, "This job is bad. I don't want it," we say, "I strongly believe that this job doesn't suit me.

I also know that there are jobs that match my interests. I will keep looking for them."

The difference between judgment and discernment may seem slight or unimportant. Yet our approach makes a profound difference in the Divine guidance we receive. When we clear judgments from our minds, we receive clearer discernment, which is another term for Divine guidance.

How to Clear the Mind

I've studied various ways to clear the mind of judgments. The most efficient method I've come across begins with understanding that all judgment stems from projection. In other words, what I judge about you is what I see within my own self. If I'm upset because I judge a person to be selfish, it's because I don't want to see or heal my own selfishness. I once believed there were exceptions to this absolute rule of projection, but time and again, I find that it's true.

However, this rule also holds great benefits for us. Since what we see in others mirrors our own self-concepts, we can use our judgments as a monitor. Whenever someone "pushes your buttons," you know that you have discovered an unclear part of your own mind. It is not possible for someone to control your emotions, only to remind you of some part of yourself over which you feel out of control.

Even if you don't entirely believe this explanation, I'd like to ask you to engage in a little experiment. The next time someone upsets you, use this exercise:

1. Stop whatever you are doing and take a deep breath.

2. If possible, close your eyes briefly and get into a comfortable sitting position.

3. Mentally say, "I am willing to release that part of me that irritates me when I think of you."

Of course, you're not releasing any real part of yourself. Instead, you are willing to release part of your false self—your lower-self ego—reflected in the mirror of the person who irritated you. Just by saying this sentence, God and the angels are given permission to lift your unwanted thoughts and beliefs. After twelve years of psychological training and thousands of clinical hours, I've yet to find a better method for clearing judgmental cobwebs from the mind.

Tapping into the Universal Intelligence

With a cleared mind, you are more receptive to the broadcast of great ideas that comes from heaven. The spiritual world tells me that deceased scientists, writers, inventors, and other thinkers conduct studies in their areas of expertise. They then look for willing men and women who would benefit from this newfound wisdom.

The deceased intellectuals deeply want to help us on earth with their discoveries. They also want to fulfill their own Divine life-purposes from the other side, since some of them missed the mark while alive. So they freely give information to living intellectuals, which may come as a sudden thought or dream. I frequently feel the presence of one of my favorite (deceased) authors, and I know that he helps me with writing projects.

Whether you desire to contact scientists and authors in the spirit world, or you simply want to have God's infinite wisdom transferred into your mind, clearing your mind of judgments is a logical starting point.

One of the best descriptions of claircognizance I have ever read appears in Napoleon Hill's classic book, *Think and Grow Rich*: The late Dr. Elmer R. Gates, of Chevy Chase, Maryland, created more than two hundred useful patents, many of them basic, through the process of cultivating and using the creative faculty . . . . Dr. Gates was one of the really great, though less publicized, scientists of the world.

In his laboratory, he had what he called his "personal communication room." It was practically sound proof, and so arranged that all light could be shut out. It was equipped with a small table, on which he kept a pad of writing paper. When Dr. Gates desired to draw on the forces available to him through his creative imagination, he would go into this room, seat himself at the table, shut off the lights, and concentrate on the known factors of the invention on which he was working, remaining in that position until ideas began to "flash" into his mind in connection with the unknown factors of the invention.

On one occasion, ideas came through so fast that he was forced to write for almost three hours. When the thoughts stopped flowing, and he examined his notes, he found that they contained a minute description of principles which had not a parallel among the known data of the scientific world. Moreover, the answer to his problem was intelligently presented in those notes. Dr. Gates earned his living by "sitting for ideas" for individuals and corporations.[1]

In his twenty-year study of the world's greatest inventors and businesspeople, Napoleon Hill found that, as he said, the "geniuses"[2] were those who tapped into the "infinite intelligence."[3] In other words, you needn't be a genius to get genius-level inspirations; you simply need to be aware and receptive.

Meditation and Sitting for Ideas

Gates' "sitting for ideas" is a form of meditation that any claircognizant can learn to use. Meditation simply means eliminating the pressure on and limits of your thinking with a calm mindset that can see things from the long view. Meditation puts us into a state where we gain new perspectives and insights about ordinary situations.

There are many excellent ways to learn about or begin a meditation program. Books, classes, and tapes abound on the topic in nearly every bookstore and metaphysical center. Even simply sitting in a comfortable position, closing your eyes, and taking a few deep breaths is enough to yield some benefits of meditation. Whenever you take a time-out from the world, you give your mind and body a well-deserved break.

In formal meditation programs, you learn to monitor your thoughts and notice the lower self's negative thought-patterns as they occur. Eastern approaches to meditation ask that you simply observe these thoughts without struggling or judging them. The spiritual healing approaches ask you to go one step further and release these thoughts to God and your guardian angels. The point is to clear your mind of distractions.

Opening Your Claircognizant Chakra

Claircognizance has an internal energy center, or chakra, corresponding to the process of receiving information from the Divine spiritual realm. Just as clairvoyance corresponds to the third eye chakra and clairaudience corresponds to the ear chakras, claircognizance corresponds to the crown chakra.

The crown chakra spins clockwise, like a ceiling fan, at the inside of the top of the head. It is the fastest-spinning chakra in the interior body, and glows in a beautiful high-vibrating shade of purple. This energy center operates efficiently when we take care of it by meditating and cleansing it of lower-self ego thoughts.

However, the crown chakra becomes clogged when we hold judgments and darkened thoughts about fear, anxiety, judgment, or distrust. Such thoughts act like greasy sludge that slows the spinning motion of the energy center. When this happens, our concentration is impaired and our thoughts are foggy.

Even if you're not quite sure you believe in chakras and meditation, it can't hurt to give chakra cleansing a try. This powerful meditation works quickly to cleanse and balance the crown chakra, whether or not you believe in its efficacy.

I first began practicing chakra-cleansing meditations after lear-ning about them in an undergraduate psychology course. No one told me that this process automatically leads to heightened psychic experiences, which I discovered quite accidentally when I began spontaneously receiving mental information, to which I wouldn't normally be privy. Strangers' life histories, facts about companies with which I worked, and accurate future events, poured into my mind.

I researched how I had received such varied and yet accurate information. I discovered that my daily chakra meditations were the catalysts. Once I understood this connection, the process of claircognizance became manageable.

Meditation to Cleanse and Balance Your Crown Chakra

You may want to tape-record the following meditation and listen to it once or twice daily:

1. After getting into a comfortable position with eyes closed, breathe in deeply through your nose. Hold the breath momentarily, then exhale slowly through your mouth. Take another deep breath, hold it, and exhale. Continue to breathe in and out at a deep and comfortable level throughout this meditation.

2. Focus on the area at the inside of the top of your head. See or feel a beautiful spinning purple fan with overlapping blades. This is your crown chakra. Take a deep breath and send the air's energy core, which is golden-white light, to the crown chakra. As you breathe in and out, more and more golden-white light surrounds your crown chakra.

3. See or feel this light dissolve all dark and negative energy attached to your crown chakra. If you like, you can mentally call the angels to help you carry away old thought patterns that do not suit your current life and ideals for yourself. The angels know which thoughts do not serve you. They simply need your permission to carry them away.

Mentally say to the angels, "I ask that you help me to cleanse away all ego thoughts that do not serve me, God, or the world."

4. *As you become willing to release these thought patterns, you see or feel the angels carry them away.* You need do nothing but be willing to be cleansed. So, be willing to release to the angels all fears that keep you from receiving Divine guidance. Be willing to release any fears about receiving new ideas.

5. *With a deep breath, be willing to release any fears about communicating with God, including fears of being controlled, manipulated, punished, or restricted.* Be willing to release any old unforgiveness you may hold toward God, including unforgiveness from the thoughts that God didn't answer your prayers or that He allowed you or a loved one to suffer, or the belief that He loves other people more than He loves you. Allow the angels to cart away from you any residual hurt or anger you may have toward members of organized religions. With another deep breath, allow the angels to clear you of any false beliefs or thoughts completely that keep you from enjoying your natural ability to communicate with God's infinite love and intelligence.

6. *Give thanks to the angels, and ask that they continue to clear away this area.* As you bring your focus back into the room, you may want to stretch or hug yourself. You'll notice that you feel wonderfully alive, alert, and refreshed. Your mind is perfectly focused and receptive to brilliant new ideas.

With your crown chakra cleansed, you will automatically notice a greater influx of claircognizant ideas and inspirations. It's a good idea to log these instances into a Divine guidance journal or a tape recorder. Often, claircognizance gives us seeds of ideas that can be the start of an entirely new venture or lifestyle. Capture those ideas as they come to you, since they are often so profound they are soon forgotten if not recorded on paper or tape.

Don't be surprised if you receive a steady influx of exciting ideas. Pray about which of these ideas to follow, and ask heaven to surround you with the courage and wisdom to put these inspirations into action. Remember, Divine guidance doesn't just give us an idea and then leave us to sink or swim on our own. God and the angels provide us with all of the support, time, money, and intelligence that we need to carry through with our guidance. All we need to do is ask for help.

In the next chapter, we'll go into specific ways to steer your claircognizant Divine guidance in your desired direction.

CHAPTER NINETEEN

❦

Experiencing Claircognizance for Yourself

You can train your mind to receive information and ideas from the infinite intelligence of the Divine mind. With a little practice and your firm commitment to receive Divine inspiration, you will have a steady flow of useful ideas and insights. You can learn how to quickly distinguish between true Divine guidance and mere imagination. No matter what your intellectual or educational background, you can be fully claircognizant.

Everyone has the ability to receive claircognizant guidance. You may believe you are not claircognizant because, in the past, you have tried too hard to receive Divine ideas and inspiration. Most people find that when they deliberately *try* to receive Divine information, they get either no information, or false information from their imagination. Claircognizants often mistakenly conclude that they are at the mercy of their mind's whims; the problem doesn't lie in their effort but in the tension and fear that surrounds their attempts.

Claircognizance Exercise 1

1. It is essential to precede your claircognizance sessions with relaxation techniques. These needn't be exotic or time-consuming rituals; merely breathing in and out deeply, shutting the eyes, and being in a distraction-free environment is enough.

2. Remember not to force ideas to appear in your mind. As mentioned earlier, any process involving struggle or strain always blocks Divine communication. You've undoubtedly experienced this yourself when you've tried hard to remem-ber a name, telephone number, or word. Only later, after you let go was your mind able to retrieve the information. With new creative projects, the same easy-does-it approachapplies.

The following questions are designed to elicit claircognizant experiences. As you receive the information, you may receive it simultaneously through other Divine communication channels: vision, hearing, and feeling. This is fine, if it happens, since the more Divine channels you have open, the better.

Breathing deeply and mentally deciding, "I am now focused and my mind is clear," are two ways to ensure a clear transmission.

3. Read and then mentally repeat each question two or three times. If doubts about your ability to receive claircognizant information enter your mind, ask the angels to clear them away for you. They will gladly take away all insecurities at your request. After all, clearing your mind is one of the angels' favorite ways to serve God.

Address these questions to God, your higher self, and the angels. Write down the thoughts, ideas, and concepts that enter your mind in response to each question.

- What thoughts do you have about how I can be more energetic during the day?

- Please tell me what career you think I would enjoy the most.

- What ideas that have come to me recently do you suggest I spend time working on?

- How can I improve my ability to concentrate and focus?

- What is the biggest block to happiness that I need to overcome in my life right now?

Claircognizant answers come as a knowingness. The information suddenly just appears, without knocking on the door or making a sound as it enters your mind. It reminds me of the magicians who appear in a flash of light on the stage.

With each question, you will notice an influx of information. Usually, the information contains thoughts that you have held before, but this time, they appear with greater clarity and focus. The reason is that your questions were sharp, clear, and focused.

Claircognizance Exercise 2

Anytime that you desire claircognizant guidance, simply use this three-step process:

1. Relax by taking a few deep breaths.

2. Decide on the question for which you truly desire an answer, and about which you are open to receiving new information.

3. Ask the question in a precise way, so that you will receive a precise answer. For example, if you desired to receive Divine guidance about your work life, you would word the question to God in a way that truly reflected your underlying desires. Since God responds to the prayers of your heart, not to what comes from the mouth and mind, the precise wording is for your own benefit. It ensures that you won't ask about Topic A and then receive an answer about Topic B (the topic that was truly in your heart). It's like computer programming, which requires absolute precision in its instructions to elicit specific results. It's the universal law of cause and effect that says, "Whatever you ask for, you will receive." The questions that God responds to come from the heart, not the head.

Heart-to-Heart Conversations with God

You can also ask for claircognizant guidance by having a heart-to-heart conversation with God and the angels. Pour out every concern you have, and God will discern the questions imbedded in your conversation. It doesn't matter whether we word the questions to Him in a formal or even polite manner. Many people receive their greatest Divine insights while angrily asking God, "Why have You let me down?" At such moments, you feel you have nothing to lose, and so you more easily tell God about your real desires. The only criteria for receiving Divine guidance are your *sincerity* about what you are asking for and your *openness* to knowing God's reply.

Being open to God's reply means you must be willing to receive an answer different from the one you expect. Sometimes we block Divine guidance because we expect God to give us one set of answers and instead receive another.

JUDY

A woman named Judy was experiencing some problems in business: her sales were down and she worried how she'd meet her monthly expenses. So she prayed for Divine guidance. Judy expected to receive practical advice, such as "Have a sale" or "Advertise in a certain newspaper." So, at first she was closed to the reply that came to her, "Love your customers more." But every evening when Judy prayed for help, she received the same idea, "Love your customers more."

When she was finally desperate for cash-flow, Judy thought, "What the heck? I'll try it!" She consciously poured out love in her thoughts and actions, going out of her way to help her customers without pushing them to buy something in the store. Her loving attitude obviously had a profound impact, because her sales increased the first day. The instant success reinforced her behavior, and the next day, she gave away free treats to her customers as she continued pouring out loving thoughts and energy. By the end of two weeks, Judy's business was stronger than ever.

Claircognizance Exercise 3

Now you can try to experience claircognizance related to items in the back of this book.

1. As you ask the questions below, take a few deep breaths to clear your mind of all distractions. Focus on each question, so you will receive an answer to only that question. Wait until you've answered all four questions before turning to the back of the book.

- What is the topic of the sentence on page 279 in the back of this book?

- Please tell me what single-digit number appears on page 280.

- What shape appears on page 281?

- What type of vehicle is described on page 282?

2. After you ask each question, take another deep breath. This action relaxes the body and quiets the mind long enough for you to be more aware of novel thoughts coming into consciousness.

Trust what you receive. You can distinguish true from false guidance by remembering that true guidance has a positive, you-can-do-it tone, whereas false guidance is pessimistic. True guidance asks you to help others, while false guidance always involves schemes to glorify your ego and make you a hero. True guidance wants to help you reach your highest potential, while false guidance wants you to beat other people in a race to the finish line. Essentially, true Divine guidance is love-based, while false guidance is rooted in fear.

3. Then, write the thoughts on paper, even if they seem illogical.

4. Later, when you've answered all four questions, compare your answers with what is in the back of the book; you'll see the logic behind your Divine guidance. Remember, you cannot fail to receive Divine guidance, because you're not the one giving it. God gives Divine guidance, and God never fails. Trust God. God loves to help us learn how to receive Divine guidance, so do not worry that the preceding questions are too trivial for Him.

5. Focus on the similarities between the answers you've written and what appears in the back of the book. This positive focus is the easiest way to gain confidence in your abilities, which is a key factor in accurately interpreting the Divine guidance you receive. If instead, you criticize yourself for the parts of Divine guidance that you misinterpreted, you will distrust the true guidance you did receive.

The main reason why people get the "wrong" information when answering claircognizant questions is that they tried too hard. As stated earlier, we strain because we are afraid, and fearful mindsets put us into our lower-self egos, which give false guidance. In other words, our "wrong" answers come from being afraid. Deep breathing and asking God and the angels to remove fears are the quickest ways I know to center our minds in love instead of fear. Also, remember God's infinite patience, and apply that same loving principle to yourself.

Claircognizance Exercise 4

Claircognizance makes you naturally gifted at discerning information about other people. When claircognizance is awakened through exercises such as those in this chapter, you can easily predict how others will act or what they will say. Did you know that you can take this skill a few steps further, and receive Divine guidance that will help you in all of your personal and business relationships?

Here is a method that gives you instant, Divinely guided information about any person in your life.

1. Quiet your mind and body by taking a few deep breaths and closing your eyes.

2. *Choose one family member, friend, or acquaintance about whom you'd like to receive Divine guidance.* It can also be a person whom you've never met in person, such as a person with whom you do business over the telephone, or an Internet acquaintance.

3. *Think about that person, and ask God and the angels:*

- What would you like me to know about this person?

- Is this person experiencing any challenges right now?

- If so, what is this person truly afraid of?

- How can I best help this person?

4. *You may want to write down the answers as you receive them.* In this way, you can study how your Divine guidance influences your relationship. You can ask these same four questions about any person. The next time a breaking news event captures your attention, try asking for Divine guidance about the people involved. You'll find that you can receive a lot of information about people whom you have never met and may never meet.

God and the angels give you any information that will help you love more and fear less. They know that if you truly understand other people, you are less apt to misjudge and more apt to hold loving thoughts.

Occasionally, the spirit world will block your access to "reading" another person. You will either get no information in response to your questions, or you will receive a thought in reply such as "It's best that you do not know right now" or "More will be revealed to you later." Either way, you'll know that God and the angels, in their infinite wisdom, are providing for everyone's needs with kindness and love.

Claircognizance Exercise 5

You can also receive claircognizant guidance while you sleep. This is an especially good way to gain new understandings and creative ideas when your daytime thinking mode is locked into black-and-white viewpoints. While sleeping, we let go of rigid thought-patterns, and God and the angels can more easily transfer Divine ideas to us when our minds are open.

Before going to bed, take a moment to meditate. Then say the following mentally or aloud:

P R A Y E R

TO ASK FOR GUIDANCE THROUGH DREAMS

Dearest God,

Please enter my dreams tonight and give me guidance and
new ideas about (fill in the blank with your specific request)
situation. I ask that You help me to remember these ideas
clearly on awakening.

Thank You and Amen.

Even if you don't normally recall your dreams, this powerful affirmation will shift your consciousness so you have vivid and unforgettable dreams during the hour immediately before awakening. These "lucid" dreams are like being in a movie, where you are simultaneously watching yourself and being the participant. It is very difficult to forget these dreams; even the person who swears they don't dream remembers the plot and the message of lucid dreams.

Many great inventions, books, and insights were derived from dreams. You've probably heard stories of authors, businesspeople, and inventors awakening with a key idea. *Everyone* has access to this pool of information, because everyone's mind is eternally joined with the infinite wisdom of God.

Jacquelyn Mitchard, the best-selling author, had a vivid dream in which she received the entire plot of a story, complete with character names. She wrote down the contents of the dream, and then set the notes aside. A year and a half later, Jacquelyn turned the notes into five chapters and sent them to a literary agent. The agent loved the book and sent it on a Friday to the editors of major publishing houses. On Monday, Jacquelyn's agent called to say that Viking Publishers was offering one-half million dollars for a two-book contract. Jacquelyn and her agent accepted the offer.

The book, *The Deep End of the Ocean,* was an instant best-seller. Then Oprah Winfrey chose it as the first book to be featured on the Oprah's Book Club. Jacquelyn's book immediately shot to the number-one spot on *The New York Times* best-seller list.

You too can work in your sleep by setting your intentions before going to sleep. You'll increase your nocturnal productivity even more by avoiding stimulants or depressants at night. These include alcohol, caffeine, nicotine, chocolate, sugar, mood-altering herbs, and any prescription or nonprescription drug that alters moods or energy levels. Also, avoid rigorous exercise within three hours of bedtime, as it elevates your body's temperature and interrupts sleep patterns.

As you drift off to sleep, say the affirmative prayer printed on page 240 of this chapter. Use this affirmation every evening for at least five nights. It's a good idea to keep a notepad or tape recorder on your nightstand to record your dreams on awakening. Within five days, the brilliant ideas you dream up will delight you.

CHAPTER TWENTY

⋘

Advanced Methods for Clearing the Divine
Communication Channels

Throughout this book, I emphasized the power of meditation combined with chakra clearing to open the channels of Divine guidance. I've also discussed how prayer can help you clear away fears and doubts, and instill faith and confidence in your Divine guidance.

Just these two methods will dramatically increase the clarity and volume of messages you receive from God and the angels. Once you become comfortable with having Divine conversations, you may, like many of us, begin asking God additional questions, such as:

- How can I receive even clearer and more understandable messages from You?

- What changes can I make in my lifestyle, right now, that will help me to more easily receive Divine guidance?

In response to these questions, God and the angels gently guide us to purify our thoughts and our bodies so we become crystal-clear instruments of Divine communication. Just as a piano serves the music better when it is well-cared for and well-tuned, so too our bodies and minds serve the spirit better when they are well-cared for and well-tuned.

When I first asked God and the angels for advanced methods to increase the understandability of my Divine guidance, I received visions of chicken meat in reply. I kept rejecting the vision as a product of my imagination, since it made no sense to me. Finally, I asked God for clarification, "Why do You keep showing me chicken meat every time I ask how I can increase the clarity of my Divine communication channels?"

The reply I received clairaudiently bowled me over. I heard, "Stop eating chicken. When you eat chicken, you are absorbing the pain that it felt when it was killed. This energy of pain is blocking your awareness of Divine guidance."

This answer stunned me. Never did I connect my diet with my receptivity to Divine guidance! Certainly, I'd noticed that after I quit drinking alcohol, my mind had become laser-sharp, and all of my abilities to concentrate, including those connected to Divine guidance, had instantly improved. But chicken meat?

I spoke to some advanced students of spirituality, and they told me that they'd received similar guidance. They had adopted a vegetarian lifestyle because they wanted to be clearer channels of Divine communication. I wanted that, too! I had given up red meat many years earlier, and primarily ate fish and fowl at my meals. I decided to follow my Divine guidance and give up all chicken and turkey.

When I stopped eating fowl, my clairvoyance changed completely, from being the equivalent of a twelve-inch black-and-white television screen, to a full-color, wide-screen television. The change was instant and dramatic. I gladly shifted to a vegetarian lifestyle in exchange for greater clarity in my Divine communications. If I *wanted* to eat a steak or a turkey drumstick, I certainly would allow myself to do so. After all, I don't believe God wants to deprive us of anything. Yet I have not wanted to eat meat, or fowl, or drink alcohol, because it's so much more fun to receive clear Divine guidance regularly!

I continued asking for advanced methods of receiving clearer Divine messages, and over time, the angels gave me the ten life-changing lessons that follow. As I put each lesson into practice, I felt lighter, freer, and happier, and my channels of Divine guidance became increasingly clearer and more enjoyable:

1. *Live in integrity.* "*Spend your time doing activities that match your highest intentions. Let go of things that your intuition prompts you to surrender. Those things may be healed so you enjoy them, or else the activity will easily drop away.*"

I cringed when the angels told me this lesson. As mentioned earlier, I was then employed by several magazines that paid me handsome wages to write articles about topics that were meaningless to me. My heart wanted to write books and articles about spiritual topics, but I feared I couldn't make a living doing what I loved.

Still, the angels urged me to trust my heart. They assured me that I would be safe to turn down work that didn't match my true interests. The first time I said no to a magazine editor's assignment to write an article I didn't care about, I felt elated. That same week, a publisher purchased a proposed book of mine about spirituality!

2. *There is only now.* "*You are complete and whole now. Don't cast your eyes on what tomorrow may bring—this implies you are imperfect or lacking now, and that you will be whole when something external comes into your life in the future.*"

When the angels sent me this lesson, I realized that I had been unconsciously living for the future. I focused on what tomorrow would bring me instead of being aware of the many blessings in my life. I changed my viewpoint by making a mental "gratitude list" each night, in which I thanked God for all of the wonderful gifts that had come to me throughout the day.

3. *All conflict is inside your mind.* "*Any conflict you see or experience in the outside world is a projection of your ego. In truth, the world is completely at peace; you project your fear of peace onto the world.*"

You don't want to resolve your inner conflict, but you do want to get it away from yourself. So you project it onto other people and think that they are the ones who are causing you discomfort. Other people are blank slates that you color with your own meanings and definitions. Then you react to them as if these colorations were real. Other people, in turn, treat you the way that you expect them to, in a self-fulfilling prophecy."

As the angels explained that I was the artist of my life's canvas, I felt both inspired and dejected. I realized how often I had allowed fear to create miserable times for me. Sometimes I feared giving and receiving love because I worried about being hurt or controlled. Other times, I created crises because I expected problems to occur. But always, as the angels pointed out to me, I was in the driver's seat. I had the power to choose the thoughts and feelings I ascribed to all situations. I had the power to listen to my intuition, which was always available to warn me of impending negativity or danger. I had the power to create problems by cultivating worry and fear. I realized I have never been the victim of outside circumstances, and with this realization I became very conscious of my expectations and choices.

4. Purify your diet. "All food has vibration, and you want to vibrate at the highest frequency to which you are attuned. Eat a diet of fresh fruits and vegetables, nuts, and whole grains; these foods have the highest frequencies. Avoid meat, dairy, alcohol, sugar, chocolate, and caffeine. And remember that the essence of all foods you eat affects you long after the food is digested and gone."

At the time that the angels told me the above lesson, my diet was already quite healthful. I had given up meats, fowl, and alcohol. Still, there was room for improvement, so I followed my guardian angel's dietary advice and adopted a vegan approach to eating. The improvement in my energy and outlook was drastic and immediate! I did not feel deprived of sugary, fat-filled, and caffeine-laden foods and beverages; rather choosing healthful foods felt easy and natural. Not once after changing my eating habits did I feel sorry for myself, as I had when dieting in the past. My angelic nutritionists shifted my eating patterns so gradually that I barely missed the foods I no longer ate.

5. Don't give in order to get. "*Let go of outlining the results that you expect from giving. You will get results from giving; that is the universal law. But it is not up to you how the cause and effect will be allocated. Plus, if you expect something in return, you haven't truly given away anything. Instead, you're holding it in consciousness, expecting to get something first before you fully release it.*"

Once again, I felt embarrassed as the angels saw into the depths of my soul. They knew that I was a giving person. Yet I had to admit the many times I'd given with expectations of receiving something in return. With full trust in my guardian angels, I decided to let go of all strings attached to my gifts to others. Almost immediately, I began receiving surprising rewards, such as new business opportunities and wonderful experiences with friends.

I learned that giving is truly its own reward, since it yields immediate joy and satisfaction. When we give, we create an outward energy that, through the law of cause and effect, always results in our receiving something of equal or greater measure. Sometimes our reward comes in unexpected ways. I noticed that, after I'd give some of my time or energy to Person A, I'd later receive some unforeseen gift from Person B. If I had stubbornly insisted on receiving a reward from Person A, I might have missed the gift from Person B. As with the other lessons, the angels immediately reinforced this lesson and it became a permanent part of my life.

6. Spend time alone in nature. "*Sounds and smells of nature are invisible, so they take your mind to the invisible realm of spirit, where things vibrate higher and faster than matter. There are healing properties in nature. Also, there are very real nature angels. You can ask these nature angels to heal you. Being in nature helps you to adapt to the natural rhythm of the earth, and since timing and cycles are a part of everything, you become more in sync with the rhythm of life."*

At the angels' urging, I ventured away from my desk more and began spending my lunch hour outdoors, even on cloudy days. Alone in nature, I hear myself think more clearly. I love feeding birds and listening to their cheery songs. The fresh air, the sunshine, and the fragrance of flowers all help me to meditate on deeper levels. If I ever feel worried or afraid, I sit outside and ask the nature angels to surround me. I feel a little like Gulliver, surrounded by the little people of Lilliput. Nature angels exude a loving energy, which feels like a giant hug from heaven.

7. Detach from matter. "When you are attached to matter in thought, you stay attached to the products of the ego mind, and thus stay attached to the ego. There is no way of escaping this law. Mind on matter is the ego mind."

My guardian angels made it clear that there is nothing wrong with material items, because matter is neutral. The angels also realize that we humans have material needs, such as food, clothing, and shelter. However, when we obsess about material items, we are focused on only our lower-self nature. And since the lower self is riddled with pain and fear, we experience these sensations by centering our thoughts on the material. I came to understand that I could let go of worries about money, and stay centered by following my intuition and the joy of my heart. This higher-self focus naturally led me to activities that resulted in my material needs being met. And it was a lot more fun than my previous outlook!

8. Judge not. "You judge others as a way of protecting yourself, to keep them away from you so you won't get close to them and get hurt. But we have told you that you don't need to think about your safety. You are safe, and an overwhelming thought pattern of concern about your safety can bring the very thing you fear into your life."

On this point, several of my guardian angels chimed in. They explained that we draw to us whatever we think about. If I obsessively think about physical or emotional danger, I create a climate in which my worst fears come true. With practice, I began noticing the moment when I'd judge other people, and then analyzing my true motivations for holding a judgment. As usual, my angels were correct! I discovered that fear was always the culprit. I began releasing my fears to the angels, and felt my judgmental habits gradually disappear. Now, if I need to be warned about some person or situation, my angels loudly tell me, and I no longer need to guard myself.

9. You live where your consciousness is focused. "If you think an unloving thought or a thought devoid of love, you feel pain. You are your consciousness and you feel the effects of where your consciousness is focused. You do not want pain. Therefore, choose to give your unloving thoughts to the light."

At first, this lesson was painful for me to face. I'd always thought that my outer circumstances influenced my happiness. The angels insisted that this was backward, and that my thoughts colored my world. They told me that my happiness didn't hinge on what I had, but instead on what I thought. I began to see the wisdom behind the adage "You can't afford the luxury of a negative thought." I began consciously avoiding negative information from television, radio, and other news media, and conversations involving gossip. Soon I had a healthy new habit of seeing the bright side of life, and in so doing, I found myself living a lighter and brighter life.

10. In all things, give glory to God. "Seek not glory for yourself. In essence, though, when you give glory to God, you are giving glory to that part of yourself that is one with God. By giving glory to God, you stay out of your ego state, and stay centered in your higher-self consciousness."

The angels had saved a most important lesson for last, the importance of letting go of all desires for praise. *"When you desire to be special, you are saying you want to be separated from God and other people,"* the angels explained. *"You will feel afraid, lonely, and in pain as a result of seeing yourself as separate."*

I learned from the angels that God is the source of all my creative energy. So anything I do or say that elicits praise should rightfully be credited to God. At first, this lesson humbled me. But before I could slip into feelings of shame, my angels boosted me with the reminder that, since my true self is one with God, I was praising the real me every time I gave glory to God.

This revelation helped me to see myself and others through the eyes of our angels. For these heavenly beings see us as we truly are: loving and creative people who desire to do the very best that we can. Yes, we occasionally make mistakes. But when we forgive ourselves and each other, we see the true beauty that is our essential nature now and always.

The ten lessons are now ingrained and permanent parts of my daily living. When my clients compliment me about the clarity of the Divine guidance I receive during our sessions, I say, "Thank you, but all credit goes to God and the angels. They taught me how to receive Divine guidance. I deserve credit merely for following that guidance, because, thanks to them, I'm now a very good listener."

CHAPTER TWENTY-ONE

Co-creating with God

We are naturally creative because of God. This makes sense, because God is our Creator, and He is continually creating. We, who are made in the image and likeness of the eternal Creator, are also eternally creative. In other words, we *can't not* create.

Every minute of every day, we create. Just like God, we create with our thoughts. Whatever we think about comes about in our experiences.

Intent Is Everything

The angels continually tell me, "Intent is everything." What you intend is what you will experience. Our intention means our mental and emotional focus, combined with our expectations. If you intend to experience pressure, stress, and lack, then you will create exactly that experience. If you intend to blame others for your troubles, then you will create that experience. If you intend to experience health, happiness, wealth, or anything else, you will create those conditions.

I remember a time in my life when I felt overwhelmed by bills. Although I didn't like the outpouring of money that went toward debt and interest payments, I didn't take any steps to resolve the situation. I just grumbled and allowed the situation to continue, as though I were a victim.

One day it occurred to me that I didn't have to live that way. I realized that I could reduce or eliminate my outstanding debt, and take control of how many bills arrived in my mailbox. By setting a firm intention to reduce my debts, I took definitive action. This intention was like picking a destination on a map, while before, I had been driving my car aimlessly. My behavior changed dramatically as I paid off larger portions of my debt and reduced my spending. Within one month, my financial situation had improved because, for me as for everyone, our intentions create our experiences.

We set our intentions every minute of every day by choosing what we want and what we expect. If we do not like what we are experiencing, we can change our intentions, and one of the easiest methods to change habitual negative intentions (such as poverty-consciousness or feelings that success is not deserved) is prayer.

I meet many people who tell me that they are aware of their habit of pushing away opportunities and success. They tell me, "I just don't feel, deep down, that I deserve to be happy." Of course, no person or circumstance can *make* us happy—that only comes from feeling love for yourself and everyone else, including God.

Still, during this life on earth, we have material needs. There is nothing wrong, immoral, or unspiritual about having enough money to take care of yourself and your loved ones.

Happily, God intends for us to be joyful and loving. Just like any loving parent, He wants the best for his beloved children. And *you* are definitely one of God's beloved children! He no more wills for you to suffer than you would want your own offspring to suffer.

If we kept our thoughts perfectly aligned with God's intentions for us, then our experiences would always flow in beautiful order and harmony. Unfortunately, we don't usually do this—we live in mental isolation from God, and speak to Him only sporadically. Though some of us consult with God more often than others, most of us do not speak to Him continually. It is a realistic and worthwhile goal to try to talk with God and the angels throughout the day; thus, we will receive reliable and creative advice for all matters.

Partnership with God

We *co-create* with God by asking for His advice, listening to it, and then following it. Co-creation is a beautiful expression of our own Divinity. It is built on the healthful habit of regularly asking God for guidance, and then being sensitive and open to His reply. We then fearlessly complete the steps as God gives them to us in steady succession.

Through this co-creation process, beautiful experiences and goals manifest almost miraculously. Yes, they do require our effort to put God's guidance into action. But, since the actions are heaven-born, they are usually fun and exciting to fulfill. I've never had God ask me to do anything that caused me or my loved ones embarrassment or pain. That old notion of God "testing us" is just a myth. We are the only ones who test ourselves.

In the traditional goal-setting process, we come up with goals and plans on our own. We write them down, fulfill them, and usually find them to be hollow victories. That is because we built these goals on externals. We saw something outside in the world and said, "That looks like something that would make me happy."

Co-creation, in contrast, comes from an internal focus. It begins when you share your hopes and desires with God. He then helps us to formulate goals that truly will be a joy to work on. God, who is one with our higher self, inside us, is already happy. Our God-given goals are nothing more than forms for the expression of this happiness.

God is like the sun, continuously sending off rays of light. This light is His creativity, His love, and His giving nature. We, who are in His image and likeness, have inborn urges to send off rays of light as well. Any goal that we co-create with God is an expression of giving light and spreading joy.

Divine Guidance Is One Hundred Percent Reliable

As you practice the steps in this book, you will receive clearer and clearer communication from God and the angels. Heaven will never guide you to do anything frightening, but you will be asked to push yourself to your true potential. When God asks you to do something wonderful and you fear that you may fail, be certain to talk to heaven about your fears. Consult with God and the angels on every fear, hope, detail, and idea, and they will remove all obstacles and open every helpful door.

Divine guidance comes to us as part of the perfectly ordered laws of the universe. Like electricity that always turns on in response to a flipped switch, our Divine guidance is one hundred percent reliable. If you turned on a light and simultaneously shut your eyes, you'd think the electricity had failed. Similarly, if you ask for Divine guidance and then shut your communication channels, you may believe that the guidance is unreliable. Divine guidance always comes in answer to our call, but we are only aware of the guidance when we are open to receive it.

Following Your Divine Guidance

So why does Divine guidance sometimes not come true? The law of free will gives us the power to change the course of our lives. For instance, let's say you receive strong intuitive guidance to apply for a certain job. Right away, it all goes well and you get an immediate appointment. At that point, you can block the success of your Divine guidance. You can decide, "I don't deserve to have a great job with a wonderful salary," and this attitude will sour your job interview. Your Divine guidance was perfectly reliable, but your free will (and ego-self guidance) sabotaged it. However, if you stay on course with your true Divine guidance, you get reliable advice for every area of your life.

Our prayers are always answered, yet we won't receive or recognize the answers unless we are alert to them. I believe this is why faith is so important. If you have faith that prayers are always answered, you are more apt to expect and notice the answers as they appear. My friend, Pilar Pollock, learned this in a very surprising way:

PILAR

Pilar finds the actor Antonio Banderas extremely attractive. One evening, during a candle lighting prayer ceremony, Pilar began thinking about him. She didn't intentionally pray to meet Antonio, but during the course of lighting her candle, Pilar thought intently about how much she wanted to meet him.

Pilar had recently met a female writer, and they had planned to have lunch soon after the prayer ceremony. The woman called to say that she'd received a sudden freelance writ-ing assign-ment that involved conducting an interview in Baja California. She asked if Pilar wanted to reschedule their lunch, or drive with her to the interview.

Pilar had a feeling that she wanted to go, but she declined anyway, thinking of the length of the trip. When they later spoke, Pilar was crushed to discover that her friend's interview subject had been none other than Antonio Banderas him-self! After this incident, Pilar is more attuned to her prayers' answers as they present themselves to her.

If God and the angels guide us to take action, we must follow it. As I wrote earlier, Divine guidance comes in baby-step incre-ments. Once we complete step 1, God gives us step 2 to follow. We won't receive step 2 until we first complete step 1. This is where some clairsentients get stuck.

PATTY

Patty, who attended one of my workshops, told me she'd prayed to God to know her life mission. Patty received her answer in a dream that told her to write a book about a topic with which she was very familiar. The dream was so clear that Patty felt it wasn't mere wishful thinking—this was true Divine guidance.

So Patty wrote a very professional and polished book and sent the manuscript to three publishers, only to receive three rejections. Demoral-ized by the unexpected disappointment—her dream had been so clear that Patty expected everything would go smoothly—she asked me for help.

I asked her if she had prayed for additional Divine guidance. When she answered, "Yes," I asked Patty what answer she'd received. She hesitated, then explained that she'd gotten a strong feeling to post her book on the World Wide Web. I asked Patty how that was going.

"Well, I looked into getting a Web page, but that's as far as I've gotten," she replied.

I asked her if she still had the strong feeling that Divine guidance was telling her to post her book on the Web.

Patty said, "Yes, but I haven't done it yet."

We discussed how she felt stuck because she was ignoring her Divine guidance. "If you have a strong feeling to take a step, then you must complete that step before God will give you the next set of instructions," I told Patty. "Divine guidance is a little like going to a correspondence school. You have to turn in the first assignment, and then they send you the next one." Patty took a deep breath and explained that she'd felt abandoned by God on her book project. Now Patty understood that it was she who had abandoned the project by not following her clairsentient guidance.

Patty's story underscores the importance of being aware of guidance and synchronicities, especially after we have prayed for Divine guidance and intervention. When we pray for guidance, stay open for its answers, and follow the instructions God gives to us, we enjoy harmonious relationships; new opportunities that come almost effortlessly; creative insights; fun, laughter, and relaxation; and health and energy.

LINDA

Linda Fields is a spiritual counselor who knows the importance of asking for Divine guidance. Recently, Linda received strong guidance to sell her home and move to another state. The guidance told Linda that she would enjoy many personal and professional experiences in her new location.

So, without hesitating, Linda prayed for additional guidance to help her make the move. She received a strong clairsentient feeling to call a certain real-estate agent. The day after she'd made the telephone call, the real-estate agent bought Linda's home. Linda said, "It was so easy! By asking for and then following my Divine guidance, I never had any of the hassles that are usually associated with moving. I just picked up the telephone, like God told me to do, and—boom—my house was sold for a wonderful price."

Linda's entire move has been charmed in the same way because she knows that when we work in partnership with God, all things are possible. Our Divine guidance can also lead us to manifest changes that benefit many people's lives. When we trust and follow such guidance, we act as an earthly angel, and heaven sends its eternal gratitude.

JIMMY

When I first met Jimmy Twyman, author of *Emissary of Light*, we both claircognizantly knew that we would work together on some very big project, although we had no idea what that project would be. Two days later, we received Divine guidance that told us more.

We felt guided to coordinate a global peace prayer, in which we would ask people from all parts of the world to join in simultaneous prayer and meditation. We drafted a letter about our vision for the global peace prayer, asking people to join in prayer on April 23, 1998 at 6:30 p.m. Eastern Time. In the letter, we discussed the scientific basis of our peace prayer, in which scientists had discovered that group prayers change the earth's energy field. "Imagine what would happen if millions of people world-wide joined together in prayers of peace," we wrote.

Jimmy and I contacted the owners of an Internet service called Iguanamatic, who agreed to donate time and Internet space to post the letter on the World Wide Web. We sent the letter announcing the prayer vigil to a few hundred friends and acquaintances, and asked them to forward the letter to friends. We also invited people to sign their names in the guestbook of our prayer vigil website.

The prayer vigil letter was distributed through this grassroots method of friends-telling-friends, to tens of thousands of people worldwide. Within two weeks of initially meeting Jimmy, our prayer vigil's website was visited by 1,000 to 5,000 people each day. From seventy-five countries, visitors signed our guestbook and wrote about their commitment to pray with us on April 23. Church leaders, celebrities, and authors contacted us, and enthusiastically endorsed the event. The *New York Times* and other media interviewed us about the event which was by then called, "The Great Experiment."

On April 23 thousands—perhaps millions—of people from all over the world joined in fifteen minutes of unified prayer and meditation. The following weekend when Jimmy and I were speakers at a conference, we agreed that our effort was one of the most powerful events in which we'd ever participated. Both of us said that we had no idea the event would become so large, but we were glad we followed our Divine guidance.

Divine Guidance Is All-encompassing

The autobiographies of highly successful people show they use hunches, meditation, dreams, and gut feelings when negotiating business opportunities and creating new inventions. Our intuitive guidance helps us to have perfect timing when making phone calls or presenting a new product idea.

While driving to work, Divine guidance helps us know:

- What time to leave.

- What route to take.

- How to avoid traffic congestion or accidents.

- What gas station to go to.

- What time we will arrive at our destination.

- Where to find a parking space.

During business appointments, our spiritual gifts help us know:

- About the person with whom we are meeting.

- If they'll be late or early (and by how much).

- What to expect about their agenda.

In advancing your career, you can get guidance about:

- Asking for a raise.

- Calling a contact.

- Advancing a new idea.

- Changing jobs.

- Getting new education, including what school and how to pay for it.

Divine awareness gives invaluable assistance in our relationships. You can use it to:

- Tune in to your children whenever you wonder where they are or what they are doing.

- Receive information about your spouse or significant other.

- Know what to say to a friend who is in distress.

- Discern the best way to help someone without being "used."

- Stay centered and peaceful during heated discussions.

- Access creative solutions to challenges involving your personal relationships.

- Get guidance while gift-shopping for your loved ones.

In my family, where spiritual communication has always been a topic of open discussion, my mother and I tune in to one another to know the best time to telephone. Spiritual awareness is also helpful for single people who want to attract a soul mate (that's how I met my husband), or who wonder about the integrity of a new lover. Married people can check in on one another's emotions and physical states using telepathy. Studies show that elderly people have the highest levels of divine awareness, and long-married couples can wordlessly converse with one another.[1]

You can use your Divine guidance proactively to create wonderful new opportunities and situations. As you've read, Divine guidance helped me to metamorphose from an unhappy and uneducated housewife into an extremely happy professional healer. I learned that God gives us instructions on how to achieve our dreams one step at a time, in the same way a correspondence school waits until you complete your first assignment before sending you the next one.

As you engage in co-creation, use your four spiritual channels to see, feel, hear, and know your God-given goal as if you already realized it. This process is called "manifestation." Experience your desire as a here-and-now reality, complete with all the details you can imagine. *See* yourself fulfilling the goal. *Feel* yourself experiencing the excitement and joy. *Hear* yourself laughing with delight, and your loved ones saying, "Congratulations! You deserve this!" *Know* that your experiences follow your thoughts and intentions, so your goal is already manifest in spirit. *Know* that God withholds nothing that supports your holy mission.

Spiritual Exercise: Manifesting Your Divine Guidance
Here are four steps that help you to put your Divine guidance into action, so that God's will (which is one with your true self's will) can manifest into form. I have taught these steps to thousands of people during my workshops, and I constantly hear how powerful these steps are.

Please remember, that gratitude is the glue that puts the co-creation together and manifests the spiritual essence into form. So, keep the "attitude of gratitude" throughout this exercise.

1. As you hold the vision, feeling, sound, and knowingness of your God-given goal in consciousness, simultaneously bask in a feeling of gratitude. Feel the warmth of being grateful that your good is already manifest. Give thanks to God now for this good. As you waft in the intense feelings of gratitude, the emotion cleanses away all disbelief and fear that could nullify your manifestation. Stay with the gratitude and remember, "Whatsoever you ask for, believe, and it shall be given."

2. Feel or see yourself putting your God-given goal into a bubble. Put the entire scene, complete with pictures, sounds, thoughts, and feelings, into the bubble. Surround the bubble with intense gratitude, knowing that the more gratitude you feel, the faster your goal will manifest on the material plane. Make the bubble glow with any color that you find beautiful. Increase the intensity and brightness of that color.

3. Hold the picture and feeling of the bubble inside your head. Visualize or feel the bubble slowly going down the inside of your body, as though it were inside an elevator. Bring the bubble to your solar plexus, just below your stomach, and stop it there. See or feel yourself pushing this bubble straight out through your navel and into the room, as though you were launching a helium-filled balloon.

4. Let the bubble go, and see or feel it float upward to the heavenly light. Feel a sense of peaceful excitement in your belly, as if something wonderful is about to happen. It is! Feel gratitude that your manifestation is now inevitable.

You have just completed the essential steps of spiritual manifestation by imagining your goal with all four channels, surrounding it with gratitude in the here-and-now, and letting it go to God. God will now give you clear guidance, one step at a time, to bring your goal into form. During the coming hours and days, pay close attention to your clairvoyant, clairaudient, clairsentient, and claircognizant Divine guidance. It will guide you perfectly to the manifestation of your God-given desires.

Give thanks to God and the angels for the beautiful gifts they have brought you. Know that you deserve these gifts, and take them graciously. Know that as you accept these gifts, you automatically give happiness and peace back into the world. Receiving and following our Divine guidance is our purpose, our happiness, our peace, and our gift to the world!

Appendix

Note to readers: For the best results, be very careful to only look at the pages that correspond to the questions you have already asked. Focus your mind so you don't see the pages corresponding to other chapters in the book.

8

Clairvoyance Question 1

A

Clairvoyance Question 2

sunflowers

Clairvoyance Question 4

Clairvoyance Question 5

A rustic mountain cabin is barely visible through the thick covering of pine trees and colorful wildflowers surrounding it. The cabin's deep brown wood has been shellacked to a lustorus shine. One windowsill has a planter with bright red geraniums. The plant's leaves are a deep shade of green. The rain cloud above the cabin sends gentle sprinkles onto the flowers. Wild birds fly for cover as the rain comes down harder and faster. The sky darkens momentarily while the cloud drops its water on the trees. Then a ray of sunshine creates a rainbow that arches perfectly over the cabin's roof.

Clairaudience Question 1

ice cube

Clairaudience Question 3

The fireworks screamed in a high-pitched squeal as they soared into the air, followed by a large bang, or—an ear-shattering *kaboom*.

Clairaudience Question 4

$$2+2=$$

Clairsentient Question 1

The day of the horse show, Bridget felt very excited. She knew that her thoroughbred horse, Alexis, was ready. After all, Bridget had trained with Alexis for months. Alexis could run the entire course and jump every hurdle without faltering an inch. Alexis looked superb, Bridget thought to herself as she brushed the horse's reddish-brown mane. Alexis whinnied and stomped her foot as Bridget checked Alexis' shoes and white socks. Bridget had braided her tail perfectly, with ribbons matching her saddle pad. Even the weather was cooperating, Bridget noted. Maybe today would be the day that she'd bring a trophy home to place on the family mantel. Just then, she heard a man's voice over the loudspeaker announce that her event was about to begin. "This is it!" Bridget said aloud to Alexis as she swung into the saddle.

Clairsentient Question 2

4

kindness

Clairsentient Question 4

Clairsentient Question 5

Q

Claircognizant Question 1

Neil Armstrong, the *Apollo 11* commander, set foot on the moon on July 20, 1969.

Claircognizant Question 2

9

Claircognizant Question 3

Claircognizant Question 4

The airplane taxied along the runway, and then pulled into the airport terminal gate.

Chapter Notes

Preface
1. 1 Cor. 13:2, 14:1, 14:31, 14:39 (New King James Version)
2. *A Course in Miracles*, Manual for Teachers

CHAPTER ONE
You Are in Constant Contact with God
1. Foundation for Inner Peace, *A Course in Miracles* (Glen Ellen, CA, 1975) text chapt. 13, sect. XI, para. 8.

CHAPTER TWO
The Source of Divine Guidance: God, the Angels, and the Spiritual Realm
1. Matthew 28:20 (New King James Version)
2. Foundation for Inner Peace, *A Course in Miracles*, Workbook for Students (Glen Ellen, CA), lesson 107, para. 2.

CHAPTER THREE
Opening to Divine Guidance: Healing Our Relationship with God
1. Daryl J. Bem and Charles Honorton, "Does psi exist? Replicable evidence for an anomalous process of information transfer," *Psychological Bulletin*. 115 (1994) 4–18.
"Scientists Peer into the Minds' Psi," *Science News* 145, no. s (January 29, 1994): 68.
2. Dean I. Radin, "Silent shockwaves: Evidence for presentiment of emotional futures," *European Journal of Parapsychology* 12 (1996)
D. I. Radin, R. D. Taylor, and W. Braud, "Remote mental influence of human electrodermal activity: A pilot replication," *European Journal of Parapsychology* 11 (1995) 19–34.
3. Hirasawam, M. Yamamoto, K. Kawano, and A. Furukawa. "An experiment on extrasensory information transfer with electroencephalogram measurement," *Journal of International Society of Life Information Science* 14 (1996) 43–48.
4. William L. MacDonald, "The effects of religiosity and structural strain on reported paranormal experiences," *Journal for the Scientific Study of Religion* 34 (1995) 366–76.

CHAPTER SEVEN
Making the Decision to Open the Channels of Divine Communication
1. MacDonald, op. cit.

CHAPTER NINE
Seeing Clearly: Ways to Increase Your Clairvoyance
1. Plutarch, *Plutarch's Moralia* (London: W. Heinemann, 1927).
   Steve Richards, *Levitation* (London: HarperCollins, 1980).

CHAPTER TEN
Experiencing Clairvoyance for Yourself
1. Foundation for Inner Peace, *A Course in Miracles*, Manual for
   Teachers, (Glen Ellen, CA), chap. 21, v. 3–4.

CHAPTER TWELVE
Hearing Clearly: Ways to Increase Your Clairaudience
1. R. F. Quider, "The effect of relaxation/suggestion and music on
   forced-choice ESP scoring," *Journal of the American Society for
   Psychical Research* 78 (1984) 241–62.

CHAPTER FIFTEEN
Feeling Clearly: Ways to Increase Your Clairsentience
1. Quider, op. cit.

CHAPTER EIGHTEEN
Knowing Clearly: Ways to Increase Your Claircognizance
1. Napoleon Hill, *Think and Grow Rich* (New York: Fawcett World
   Library, 1960).
2. Ibid., 181–82
3. Ibid.

CHAPTER TWENTY-ONE
Co-creating with God
1. MacDonald, op. cit.

About the Author

DoreenVirtue (yes, that *is* her real name) holds B.A., M.A., and Ph.D. degrees in Counseling Psychology. The daughter of a Christian Science spiritual healer, Doreen is a fourth-generation metaphysician who grew up with miracles and angels. She blends psychology, spiritual communication, and the principles of *A Course in Miracles* in her private practice, where she conducts angel therapy and spiritual healing. Doreen gives Divine Guidance workshops and lectures across the country. She is the author of *Angel Therapy* and *The Lightworker's Way*.

For information about DoreenVirtue's "Divine Guidance" weekend courses, please call the American Institute of Hypnotherapy at 800-872-9996 or 714-261-6400 or call 800-654-5126, ext. 0. To correspond with Doreen, or to receive her complete lecture schedule, please write to Renaissance Books 5858 Wilshire Blvd., Suite 200, Los Angeles, CA 90036 or visit her website at http://www.angeltherapy.com.

Also by Doreen Virtue

Books

Angel Therapy: Healing Messages for Every Area of Your Life

The Lightworker's Way: Awakening Your Spiritual Power to Know and Heal

"I'd Change My Life If I Had More Time": A Practical Guide to Making Dreams Come True

The Yo-Yo Diet Syndrome: How to Heal and Stabilize Your Appetite and Weight

Constant Craving: What Your Food Cravings Mean and How to Overcome Them

Losing Your Pounds of Pain: Breaking the Link Between Abuse, Stress, and Overeating

Audiotapes

Chakra Clearing: A Morning and Evening Meditation to Awaken Your Spiritual Power

Losing Your Pounds of Pain (abridged)